ISAIAH

DISCOVER TOGETHER BIBLE STUDY SERIES

1 Peter: Discovering Encouragement in Troubling Times
1 and 2 Thessalonians: Discovering Hope in a Promised Future
Daniel: Discovering the Courage to Stand for Your Faith
Ecclesiastes: Discovering Meaning in a Meaningless World
Ephesians: Discovering Your Identity and Purpose in Christ
Galatians: Discovering Freedom in Christ Through Daily Practic
Hosea: Discovering God's Fierce Love
Isaiah: Discovering Assurance Through Prophecies About Your Mighty King
James: Discovering the Joy of Living Out Your Faith
Luke: Discovering Healing in Jesus's Words to Women
Philippians: Discovering Joy Through Relationship
Proverbs: Discovering Ancient Wisdom for a Postmodern World, Volume 1
Proverbs: Discovering Ancient Wisdom for a Postmodern World, Volume 2
Psalms: Discovering Authentic Worship
Revelation: Discovering Life for Today and Eternity
Ruth: Discovering God's Faithfulness in an Anxious World

Leader's guides are available at www.discovertogetherseries.com

DISCOVER TOGETHER

BIBLE STUDY

ISAIAH

*Discovering Assurance Through Prophecies
About Your Mighty King*

Sue Edwards

KREGEL
PUBLICATIONS

Isaiah: Discovering Assurance Through Prophecies About Your Mighty King
© 2022 by Sue Edwards

Published by Kregel Publications, a division of Kregel Inc., 2450 Oak Industrial Dr. NE, Grand Rapids, MI 49505. www.kregel.com.

Cataloging-in-Publication Data is available from the Library of Congress.

ISBN 978-0-8254-4762-4

Printed in the United States of America
22 23 24 25 26 27 28 29 30 31 / 5 4 3 2 1

Contents

Why Study the Bible?

Varied voices perpetually shout for our attention. Whose voice deserves our trust? The politician or evangelist on television? The Wall Street CEO? The Uber driver we've never met but count on to take us home? The man hawking cell phones behind the counter? The woman on the treadmill beside us? Maybe we can trust them; maybe we can't. Over time we can discern whether or not we're comfortable inviting them into our personal space or giving weight to their opinions. But the reality is that in time, everyone will disappoint us, and we will disappoint them too.

Only One is perfectly trustworthy. Only One offers authentic hope. "Therefore, with minds that are alert and fully sober, set your hope on the grace to be brought to you when Jesus Christ is revealed at his coming" (1 Peter 1:13).

Years ago a wise woman, who secretly paid for my daughters to attend a Christian school we couldn't afford, planted that truth in my mind and heart. This concept blossomed into realistic expectations for life and a hearty hunger for a relationship with that One trustworthy person. That hunger led to a lifetime of savoring God's Love Letter, the Scriptures, and that relationship and practice upended everything. Wherever you are in your journey, Jesus invites you to experience abundant life with him. How?

Together let's discover what the Old Testament prophet Isaiah reveals about the King and his kingdom and find courage.

How to Get the Most Out of a Discover Together Bible Study

We're all at different junctures in our spiritual journeys, but God's Word doesn't separate us according to superficial differences. We all want to know God intimately and flourish, and we can all learn from one another. "As iron sharpens iron, so one person sharpens another" (Proverbs 27:17).

Discover Together Bible studies are designed to promote unity, for all women to learn from and enjoy together regardless of age, stage, race, nationality, spiritual maturity, or economic or educational status. God proclaims we are all sisters in his forever family, preparing to spend eternity together (Matthew 12:46–50).

However, our schedules vary week to week depending on the needs of loved ones, travel responsibilities, and work demands. To honor these differences, this study provides two choices:

- Basic questions that require one to one and a half hours of prep a week, offering in-depth Bible study with a minimum time commitment.
- "Digging Deeper" questions for women who want to probe the text more deeply.

Women wanting to tackle the "Digging Deeper" questions may

- need resources such as an atlas, Bible dictionary, or concordance;
- check online resources and compare parallel passages for additional insight;
- use an interlinear Greek-English text or Vine's Expository Dictionary to do word studies;
- grapple with complex theological issues and differing views; and
- create outlines and charts and write essays worthy of seminarians.

In addition to God's Love Letter, we also need authentic community and a place to be ourselves, where we are loved unconditionally despite our differences and challenged to grow.

This Bible study is designed for both individual and group discovery, but you will benefit more if you complete each week's lesson on your own and then meet with other women to share insights, struggles, and aha moments.

If you choose to meet together, someone needs to lead the group. You will find a free downloadable leader's guide for each study, along with tips for facilitating small groups with excellence, at www.discovertogether series.com.

Choose a realistic level of Bible study that fits your schedule. You may want to finish the basic questions first and then dig deeper as time permits. Take time to savor the questions, and don't rush through the application.

Read the sidebars for additional insight to enrich the experience. Note the optional passages to memorize, and determine if this discipline would be helpful for you.

Do not allow yourself to be intimidated by women who have walked with the Lord longer, who have more time, or who are gifted differently. You bring something to the table no one else can contribute.

Make your study top priority. Consider spacing your study throughout the week to allow time to ponder and meditate on what the Holy Spirit is teaching you. Do not make other appointments during the group Bible study. Ask God to enable you to attend faithfully.

Come with an excitement to learn from others and a desire to share yourself and your journey. Give it your best to find the only One who will never let you down.

WHAT IS INDUCTIVE STUDY, AND WHY IS IT SO POWERFUL?

The Discover Together series uses inductive Bible study as a structure to dig into the Bible. Inductive study is the practice of investigating or interviewing a Bible passage to determine its true meaning, attempting to leave behind any presuppositions or personal agendas.

First, we seek to learn what the original author meant when writing to the original audience. We carefully examine the words and ideas. We ask questions like, What is happening? Who is it happening to? And where is it happening? Only after we answer those questions are we ready to discern what we think God meant.

And once we are clear about what God meant, then we are ready to apply these truths to our present circumstances, trusting that a steady diet of truth will result in an enriched relationship with Almighty God and beneficial changes in our character, actions, and attitudes.

Inductive study is powerful because discerning biblical truth is the best way we grow in faith, thrive in our lives, and deepen our relationship with the God who created us.

To experience this powerful process, we must immerse ourselves in the practice of study as a lifestyle—and not just focus on a verse here and there. Our life goal must be to digest the Bible, whole book by whole book, as life-giving nourishment that cannot be attained any other way.

Over a span of sixteen hundred years, God orchestrated the creation of sixty-six biblical documents written by the Holy Spirit through more than forty human authors who came from different backgrounds. Together they produced a unified Love Letter that communicates without error God's affection, grace, direction, truth, and wisdom. He did this so that we would not be left without access to his mind and heart (Hendricks and Hendricks, *Living by the Book*, 23).

THE INCREDIBLE BENEFITS OF BIBLICAL LITERACY

Earning a quality education changes us. It makes us literate and alters our future. Many of us sacrifice years, money, and energy to educate ourselves because we understand education's benefits and rewards.

Biblical literacy is even more valuable than secular education! But just like with secular learning, becoming biblically literate requires serious investment. However, the life-changing rewards and benefits far outweigh a diploma and increased lifetime earnings from the most prestigious Ivy League university.

A few benefits to Bible study include

- a more intimate relationship with Almighty God;
- an understanding of the way the world works and how to live well in it;
- a supernatural ability to love ourselves and others;
- insight into our own sin nature along with a path to overcome it, and when we fail, a way to wipe the shame slate clean, pick ourselves up forgiven, and move on with renewed hope;
- meaning and purpose;
- relational health experienced in community;
- support through struggles;
- continued growth in becoming a person who exhibits the fruit of the Spirit: love, joy, peace, patience, kindness, goodness, faithfulness, gentleness, and self-control (Galatians 5:22–23); and
- contentment as we learn to trust in God's providential care.

Every book of the Bible provides another layer in the scaffolding of truth that transforms our minds, hearts, attitudes, and actions. What truths wait to be unearthed in Isaiah's prophecies, and how will they change us?

Why Study Isaiah?

Do you yearn to live in a place where justice, peace, unending goodness, and joy are the "normal" state of affairs? The Bible talks about a kingdom where these things are normal. If you have placed your trust in Christ, you are already a citizen of that glorious place. The Bible calls it the millennial kingdom because it's going to last a thousand years (Revelation 20:6). And one day, possibly not that long from now, you will dwell there with his other followers. But every triumphant kingdom requires a qualified monarch, and our perfect sovereign is none other than King Jesus himself!

Enter with me into the wonder of this ancient text for a new vision of our Messiah, King Jesus, and his future kingdom.

TO INFUSE US WITH COURAGE WHILE DWELLING IN A WEARY WORLD

Twenty-seven centuries ago, Isaiah prophesied about our magnificent King and his kingdom, providing details to brighten our days when we are disheartened. Can you imagine? Isaiah's descriptions of our new country are designed to help us want to make space in our busy lives for our soon-coming King. After all, you can't have the kingdom without the King.[1] Not only is Isaiah quoted in the New Testament more than any other Old Testament prophet, but his message is also meant for us today.

TO INCREASE OUR CONFIDENCE THAT THE BIBLE IS TRUE

Biblical promises provide comfort and courage, but how do you know that God's Word is trustworthy? One of the amazing facts about Scripture is that exact details concerning Jesus and his future kingdom were predicted by prophets with astounding accuracy centuries before their fulfillment. Isaiah, named by some as the prince of prophets, was one of those prophets (Jensen, *Isaiah & Jeremiah*, 27). Andrew M. Davis writes,

Only Christianity has this gift of predictive prophecy so clearly

---

1. *Some Christians today want the kingdom without the King* is a concept based on a sermon series by the author's senior pastor, Neil Tomba, Northwest Bible Church, Dallas, Texas, fall 2020 through fall 2021.

fulfilled in the pages of history. There are no such Hindu prophecies, or Buddhist or Muslim. None of those competitors in the marketplace of ideas can point to verifiable prophecies that have been fulfilled in space and time. But Isaiah the prophet, empowered by the Holy Spirit, made hundreds of such predictions, telling things before they happened, "so that when it does happen you may believe" (John 14:29). (Davis, *Christ-Centered Exposition*, 4)

Around 760 years before the birth of Christ, the preincarnate Son of God called Isaiah to instruct Israel about God and his truths, to warn those who had walked away from their faith, and to comfort those who were trusting and following God in the midst of a hostile pagan culture. Interwoven into Isaiah's sermons and writings are beautiful predictions of the coming Messiah, King Jesus, and his thousand-year reign on the earth (the millennial kingdom), as well as prophecies about the new heavens and the new earth. Many of Isaiah's predictions have already been fulfilled, but some are still future. The amazingly accurate, already fulfilled prophecies give us confidence that future predictions of a loving, joyful kingdom are also true.

THE AUTHOR'S PERSPECTIVE ON END TIMES

Respected Bible scholars and pastors hold different views about how to interpret the Bible related to end times. Should we interpret these particular passages literally or figuratively? When will these events occur? How do all the pieces fit together?

I hold a premillennial, pretribulation view. That means I believe the end-time events will really occur in the future. Isaiah wrote about real future events. This approach consistently interprets the Bible literally, attempting to understand first what the original author was communicating to the original audience and then what that text means for us today. I hold that if the original author seemed to be using figurative language, then we should take that into account, but otherwise I believe the passage means what it says.

Some Christian doctrines are central to the faith—for example, the virgin birth, Christ's atonement, and the return of Christ—but others are disputable. That means that respected godly scholars who believe in the inerrancy of the Bible disagree on some of the details. Christians should not break fellowship with other believers on these disputable matters.

That said, prophecies about what will happen in the future are all through the Bible, and I have found them to be indescribably comforting and life giving as I navigate the complex maze of living in a fallen world. When I'm discouraged and need hope, looking ahead to the glorious future my Jesus has planned for me enables me to look up and push forward. I so desire that you experience that magnificent hope too.

THE AUTHOR'S PERSPECTIVE ON THE TERMS "HEAVEN" AND "THE KINGDOM" IN ISAIAH

In this study, I will use the terms "heaven" and "the kingdom" in light of my premillennial, pretribulation view. Thus, when I say "heaven," "the kingdom," or the other end-time terms below, here's what I mean:

Heaven: This word in Hebrew refers to the sky as well as the space beyond our atmosphere. It also can mean the unseen celestial places, God's dwelling place. The Greek term is similar and speaks of the air or sky. Where is this "heaven"? It is always referred to as "up," so we can assume it's an atmospheric place beyond our physical reach. However, many Christians envision heaven as a place where we will be floating on clouds, playing harps for eternity—but that's not a biblical concept. The Bible teaches that those of us who die before the rapture will not cease to exist. At that moment our physical body and our spirit separate. Our physical body stays on earth, but our spirit immediately goes to "heaven." In 2 Corinthians 5, Paul describes us leaving our physical bodies, our "earthly tent," and moving into a heavenly dwelling—thus the term "heaven," where our spirits are in the presence of God.

Believers alive at the rapture will enjoy a different experience. The term "rapture" means *caught up, snatched suddenly*. First Thessalonians 4:15–17 provides details:

> According to the Lord's word, we tell you that we who are still alive [at the time of the rapture], who are left until the coming of the Lord, will certainly not precede those who have fallen asleep. For the Lord himself will come down from heaven, with a loud command, with the voice of the archangel and with the trumpet call of God, and the dead in Christ will rise first. After that, we who are still alive and are left will be caught up together with them in the clouds to meet the Lord in the air. And so we will be with the Lord forever.

At the rapture, those of us who have already died physically will experience the uniting of our physical bodies with our disembodied spirits that have been waiting in "heaven" for this day. After that, living believers will immediately receive their glorified resurrected bodies and will also be caught up to meet the Lord in the air. Read 1 Corinthians 15:42–58 for the incredibly exciting details.

After the rapture, we wait back in "heaven" in the presence of the Lord for the consummation of earth's history as we know it, including the tribulation, a seven-year period of horrendous chaos and judgment on the earth (Revelation 4–19). However, out of God's divine love and mercy, followers of Jesus won't suffer through this tribulation period (1 Thessalonians 1:8–10).

During their wait, believers in their glorified resurrected bodies will experience spectacular events like the judgment seat of rewards, known as the bema seat (2 Corinthians 5:6–10; 1 Corinthians 3:10–15; 4:4–5), the marriage celebration, and the wedding supper of the Lamb (Revelation 19:6–9).

At the culmination of the tribulation, King Jesus returns to earth for a second time, also known as the second coming, and he brings us back with him to set up his millennial kingdom (Revelation 19:11–16).

The Kingdom: Whenever I refer to "the kingdom" in this study, I mean the "millennial kingdom" described in Revelation 20. The term "kingdom" has several nuanced meanings in the Bible. In one sense, when Jesus came to earth the first time, he brought aspects of the kingdom with him. We know about his righteousness and holiness that characterize the kingdom. But the Bible also reveals another kingdom that Isaiah tells us about—a glorious future kingdom that Christ will inaugurate on the earth. This is a literal one-thousand-year kingdom led by King Jesus, a place of yearned-for justice and peace.

While we are in "heaven" during the tribulation on the earth, Revelation 5:9–10 records a song we will sing to Jesus:

> You are worthy to take the scroll
> > and to open its seals,
> because you were slain,
> > and with your blood you purchased for God
> > persons from every tribe and language and people and nation.
> You have made them to be a kingdom and priests to serve our God,
> > and they will reign on the earth.

The Bible teaches that a grand future awaits God's children. This passage reveals that believers will rule and reign plus serve and lead with Christ in that glorious millennial kingdom for one thousand years. After the millennial kingdom, the Bible explains that the earth will be cremated and replaced with "a new heavens and a new earth." Read the last two chapters of the Bible for insight into our final destination, a place almost beyond comprehension. These marvelous passages are meant to encourage and inspire us. That's why in 1 Thessalonians 2:12 Paul urges all Christians "to live lives worthy of God, who calls you into his kingdom and glory."

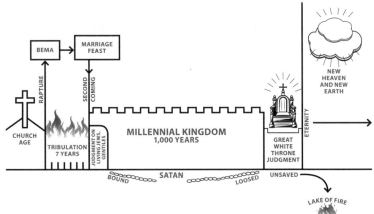

HOW TO DISAGREE AGREEABLY

Ultimately, each of us is responsible to study the related texts prayerfully and carefully and then determine what we believe the Bible teaches about our future. Some of the passages are beyond our ability to fully grasp, and we may find when we get there that none of us were 100 percent correct. However, we can know that whether our ultimate destiny is in "heaven" or in the "millennial kingdom" and then the "new heavens and the new earth" that God is good and eternity with the triune God will be glorious and forever.

Therefore, if you work through this study with others, they may express different opinions. Allow them the freedom to articulate their ideas. Listen with respect to everyone. Create a safe place where honest dialogue thrives. Trust the Holy Spirit to teach each of us as we gather to learn and encourage one another. Don't be afraid to gently disagree, but focus on the ideas and don't allow these differences to elevate into personal disputes. Love one another and refuse to sacrifice your unity over disputable matters. At the same time, speak up kindly concerning what you believe the Bible teaches and why. As we say in our seminary, "Teach truth; love well."

THE NATURE OF DIVINE PROPHETIC LITERATURE

Biblical prophets, empowered by the Holy Spirit, testify to the majesty of an all-knowing, powerful creator God who stands outside of time and moves history through a preordained, Trinity-created plan to ultimately restore the heavens and the earth to a place of peace, joy, and justice. These prophets didn't know when their prophecies would come to pass. In fact, some prophecies had double meanings—they were fulfilled in some sense quickly, and in another sense they will be fulfilled in the future.

> He [Isaiah] stood as if he were on mountaintops and looked ahead over misty mountain ranges, peak upon peak of future events. As one looks out over such peaks, they appear as if they were layered right on top of each other, though they are separated by dozens of miles. So also Isaiah could see distant future events on top of each other as if they were side by side, though they were separated by many years. (Davis, *Christ-Centered Exposition*, 3)

Isaiah's greatest prophecies pictured details concerning the key figure in history who would make the Godhead's plan possible—a member of the Trinity, the Messiah, Jesus the Christ. Centuries later many of Isaiah's prophecies came true. The Messiah was born to a virgin, lived a sinless life as a common carpenter, spent three years teaching and modeling perfect love, compassion, and justice, and died on a wooden cross to atone for the sins of all who would humble themselves and ask to be a part of his forever family.

This unfathomable sacrifice opened the door for sinful humankind to enter that family and enjoy the priceless privileges of intimate fellowship with their Creator. In addition, God's family will enjoy eternal life in Messiah's renewed millennial kingdom and the new heavens and the new earth. Also, God gave Isaiah glimpses of the splendid new homes the Lord will create for us. Although a more complete understanding of what Isaiah saw only comes through other prophecies, like puzzle pieces, revealed through the age, we are privileged to have access to thousands of these pieces in Scripture. As we put each puzzle piece into place, we gain a clearer picture of the God who loves us and the future he created for us. And as the picture becomes more complete, we enter into a deeper relationship with God, giving us the courage to release to our perfect king the anxiety and overwhelming expectations we face. God expects us to take the time to work the puzzle, and this study will be a part of that endeavor.

BACKGROUND INFORMATION

What We Know About the Prophet Isaiah

Isaiah's name means "the Lord is salvation." He was a gifted poet, statesman, preacher, and writer who lived in Jerusalem. He displayed a sharp intellect, and because he had easy access to the king, we know he grew up in a prominent family (7:3). He exhibited a bold faith, a fearless authenticity, and a masterful creativity.

He was married to an unnamed prophetess (8:3), and we can imagine that they shared a fervent passion for ministry. They had two sons, and God instructed them to give each boy an unusual name. Each name embodied major aspects of Isaiah's prophetic messages, reminding hearers of Isaiah's sermons whenever they saw the boys.

One son was named Maher-Shalal-Hash-Baz (Ma-hair-shah-la-hash-bahz), which means "quick to plunder, swift to spoil." This boy served to constantly warn Israel that if they continued to rebel against God, they would bring God's discipline upon themselves and he would allow a foreign power to take them into a harrowing seventy-year-long exile. That exile began in 701 BC, when Assyria devastated the land and carried the Jews into slavery.

The other son was named Shear-Jashub (Share-YA-shube), which means "a remnant will return." This son reminded the Israelites that even if God disciplined them by sending them into exile, a remnant of God's people would remain faithful and always return to the land of blessing.

Isaiah's World

After King Solomon died, civil war ensued, and Judah broke off from Israel to form a divided nation. The northern part of the nation kept the name "Israel," and the southern region adopted the name "Judah."

Isaiah's primary audience was Judah, especially Judah's capital city, Jerusalem, Isaiah's hometown. He ministered during the reigns of four different kings—Uzziah, Jotham, Ahaz, and Hezekiah. The political upheaval and chaos that accompanied the rise and fall of these four kings would provide fodder for a dramatic Netflix special, full of intrigue, sabotage, and unsuccessful attempts to ally with foreign nations instead of turning to the Lord for help.

During these tumultuous years, internal resentment built as the rich oppressed the poor and the religious leaders exploited the common people until many allowed their authentic faith in God to dry up into hollow ritualism. Into this crumbling society, God sent Isaiah to wake the people and call them back to a relationship with him and a lifestyle that reflected that genuine faith. If the Israelites turned a deaf ear, God would allow serious consequences to gain their attention and provoke repentance. In the first five chapters of the book, God, through Isaiah, describes Judah's putrid state of affairs.

Within Isaiah's recorded sermons and writings, glimpses of hope shine not only for the Jews but for the whole world for all time. In our study, we will focus on these magnificent prophetic signs and pictures of a glorious Messiah and our eternal future. Let's get started.

Your King Commissions Isaiah—and You

What helped Isaiah stay strong in his faith, despite being misunderstood and enduring various trials? What helped New Testament Christians persevere through similar adversity? In both the Old and the New Testaments, we see that God peppered truths about our glorious futures in eternity to inspire and encourage us to persevere. But many Christians today are unaware of the magnificent eternal rewards and blessings that await us as we honor God regardless of disappointment in this fallen world.

As you work through this study, you'll uncover truths and treasures that will fuel your days with joy and expectation. So look up. Your King is coming for you, and he's bringing his kingdom with him. When he comes, your earthly home will be transformed, as will your physical body and your daily life. It could be tomorrow. It could be the instant after you take your last earthly breath. All creation waits. Come and discover your new home in Jesus's millennial kingdom and beyond.

ISAIAH'S ADVERSITY

Isaiah experienced discouragement over the miserable state of affairs in his country. The reign and death of King Uzziah in about 740 BC caused Isaiah even more grief. Uzziah ruled for fifty-two years, and for most of those years he had been the most righteous Judean king since Solomon. However, during his later years, Uzziah turned away from God, and the Lord judged him for his disobedience and pride by striking him with leprosy. This horrific infectious disease caused extensive nerve damage resulting in the loss of part of his extremities. He was declared "unclean" and lived alone, isolated from public life, friends, and family, until his death, requiring his son Jotham to reign in his place. King Uzziah's life and death was a tragic picture of Judah's fall. Initially, Judah loved and followed God, but later she became an unfaithful nation worshipping other gods.

At this critical time in history, God sent a vision calling Isaiah to speak truth to God's people. This throne-room vision colored Isaiah's view of

> **OPTIONAL**
>
> **Memorize Romans 12:1**
> Therefore, I urge you, brothers and sisters, in view of God's mercy, to offer your bodies as a living sacrifice, holy and pleasing to God—this is your true and proper worship.

> What Michelangelo is among artists, what Beethoven is among composers, what Lincoln is among presidents, what Spurgeon is among preachers, what Lombardi and Wooden are among coaches, Isaiah is among the prophets. He is the best educated. He is the most prolific. And if quotations in the New Testament are any guide, he is the most influential. . . . But, as is true of most of the prophets, he lived a misunderstood life.
> —Charles Swindoll
> (*Swindoll Study Bible*, 805)

God for the rest of his life and ministry. However, as we'll discover in this lesson, Isaiah's vision and his response are far more than just a picture of heaven. They also reveal the steps each of us needs to take if we want God to use us significantly for him.

WHAT ISAIAH SAW

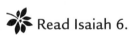 Read Isaiah 6.

1. Who did Isaiah see? How did Isaiah describe him? Who was with him? Where was Isaiah? (6:1–2)

2. The apostle John identifies this magnificent person in John 12:41. Who does John say Isaiah saw?

3. Read Mark 9:2–8, when John was privileged to see the transfigured Jesus. Describe the incident. How did the disciples react? How do you think you would have felt, and what would you have done?

4. Later in his life, John saw Jesus again in his post-incarnate state (Revelation 1:9–17). How did John react this time? What details does he include that Mark left out when describing the transfiguration?

DIGGING DEEPER

For more insight into Isaiah's world and the sorry state of Judah and its capital city, Jerusalem, read the first five chapters of Isaiah. What common themes run through these chapters? Why was Judah in need of the correcting and encouraging words of the prophet Isaiah?

DIGGING DEEPER

To learn more about King Uzziah, also known as Azariah, study 2 Chronicles 26 and 2 Kings 15:1–72. What can you learn about the priority of remaining loyal to your God throughout your lifetime?

God is the highest good of the reasonable creature, and the enjoyment of him is the only happiness with which our souls can be satisfied. To go to heaven fully to enjoy God is infinitely better than the most pleasant accommodations here. Fathers and mothers, husbands, wives, children, or the company of earthly friends, are but shadows. But the enjoyment of God is the substance. These are but scattered beams, but God is the sun. These are but streams, but God is the fountain. These are but drops, but God is the ocean.
—Jonathan Edwards ("The Christian Pilgrim," SermonIndex.net)

5. Do you think you will ever see the glorious Son and God the Father yourself (Revelation 22:3–5)? How can you be sure (1 John 5:10–12)?

6. Read 1 John 3:1–2. What are your thoughts and feelings as you savor this beautiful promise?

In a very real sense, all Messianic prophecy in the Old Testament is Kingdom prophecy. Even those predictions which deal with Messiah's humiliation and sufferings cannot be separated from the context of regal glory.
—Alva McClain (*Greatness of the Kingdom*, 217)

WHAT ISAIAH HEARD

7. What were the angels calling to one another (6:3)? How loud were their voices? What happened in the temple as a result (6:4)?

His holiness is simply his God-ness in all his attributes, works, and ways. . . . He is not like us. . . . He is in a different category. He is holy.
—Raymond Ortlund Jr. (*Isaiah*, 77)

There is something about holiness that scares us, and something about a person who claims to be holy that threatens us. People like that make us feel uncomfortable, inferior, unworthy, guilty, and condemned. The less holy we think we are, the farther away from them we want to run. . . . But the solution is not to run and hide. . . . It is to acknowledge our sin and to accept the forgiveness He has offered us in His Son.
—Richard Strauss (*Joy of Knowing God*, 127, 135)

ISAIAH'S RESPONSE

8. What did Isaiah cry out as he beheld this vision? What realization caused this outburst? (6:5)

DIGGING DEEPER

Read Luke 5:1–11 and compare Peter's and Isaiah's experiences and responses when they understood their own sin and God's holiness.

We all need more help than we think we need.
—Senior Pastor Neil Tomba (In multiple "Jesus the King" sermons)

9. During the latter part of Jesus's earthly ministry when he was teaching the crowds, some asked him questions about what would happen to people who had recently died. The governor of Judea, Pontius Pilate, had murdered some Jewish people, and a tower had fallen on others in Siloam. Jesus used these questions to teach the crowd an important lesson on recognizing their own sin and repenting. What did he teach them in Luke 13:1–5?

10. John the Baptist brought a similar message to kick off his cousin Jesus's earthly ministry. Who did John quote, and what was his main message? (Mark 1:1–4)

11. When compared to God's holiness, who needs help (Romans 3:10)? How can anyone receive God's forgiveness, and on what basis is that help given (Romans 3:21–25)?

12. What do you think it means to repent, based on the passages in questions 8–11?

13. Why do you think repentance is the precursor to receiving God's forgiveness, becoming his child, and living eternally in his kingdom? Why is awareness of our sin needed to become a follower of Jesus? (1 John 1:8–10)

14. Reread Isaiah 6:6–7. What do you think the burning coal in the angel's tongs foreshadows? How do these verses in Isaiah's vision symbolize Jesus's future mission on earth?

15. What is your personal response as you consider God's holiness? Do you need help to overcome your failures, rebellions, and shortcomings? What consequences are you reaping by not asking for help? Why not ask God for help now?

ISAIAH'S CALL

After Isaiah humbled himself and recognized his great need for help, God covered his sins with grace and called him to a life of significant purpose.

16. What two questions did God ask Isaiah (6:8)? What is unusual about the second question? What does this question teach us about the doctrine of the Trinity, that God is three persons in one essence and purpose, Father, Son and Holy Spirit?

DIGGING DEEPER

Since Jesus's sacrifice on the cross is required to cover sins, how did God cover the sins of Isaiah? Was Jesus's sacrifice retroactive, and if so, what was required for those who loved God to be saved in Old Testament times? Study Genesis 15, paying special attention to verse 6.

17. What was Isaiah's immediate response in verse 8? Has God called you to serve him in a particular way or ministry? If so, share this calling with your group.

18. If you are hesitant to move forward in your calling, can you discern and explain why? How might trusting mighty King Jesus help you?

In Isaiah 6:9–12 Jesus explained to Isaiah what his ministry would entail and how the people would respond to it. He even explained the devastating discipline that God would need to inflict on the Israelites because of their refusal to repent and turn from their wicked ways. This news disheartened Isaiah. He asked in verse 11, "For how long, Lord?" Imagine God asking you to spend your life in a ministry with little success. Yet, like Isaiah, we are never responsible for the results, only to be faithful.

Regardless of our God-given mission, these verses perplex many readers. The passage reveals that some people are a stiff-necked people with uncircumcised hearts and ears (Acts 7:51) and choose to reject God's initial overtures. The more these stiff-necked people hear, the more they harden their heart against God's message. Finally, it seems God moves to a strategy of discipline—as he did with the Judeans and Israelites—knowing they will not otherwise humble themselves and turn to God for help. Although unfathomable to us, God is not bound by time and knows the outcome of all things.

Old Testament scholar Barry Webb writes,

> Sentence has been passed on the nation in heaven; Isaiah's preaching will put it into effect on earth. Verses 9–10 indicate that the very unresponsiveness of the people will be an aspect of God's judgment on them. They have chosen arrogance and indifference; they shall have them in full measure and experience their bitter fruits: devastation and exile (12). Judgment is now inevitable. (Webb, *The Message of Isaiah*, 61)

However, none of us know when an individual has reached the point of no return. My mother resisted God for ninety-one years. The hypocrites in the town where she grew up, including the uncredentialed and untrained pastors, inoculated her against the gospel. Our family prayed for her for many years and did everything we could to show her God's love. Yet she continued to respond out of bitterness and mistrust—until three weeks before she died. Through a series of events that only God could orchestrate, and in the quiet of a hospital room with my daughter at her side, she softened her heart.

Like Isaiah, we must never give up.

GOD'S HOLY SEED IN THE STUMP

19. The Bible uses the term *remnant* in several prophetic books and also in Romans. From these verses, what do you think this term means in Scripture and how does it relate to the tenth in Isaiah 6:13?

Isaiah 11:11

Jeremiah 23:3

DIGGING DEEPER

Despite the bleak news Isaiah received regarding his future ministry, 6:13 offers hope. The first part of the verse refers to *a tenth*. What do you think Isaiah meant?

Zechariah 8:12–13

Romans 11:5

DIGGING DEEPER

Who were the initial "holy seed" (Isaiah 41:8-9; 59:20; 65:8-9; 1 Kings 19:18; Romans 11)? Who is the ultimate "holy seed" who would come forth out of chastened Israel and Judah?

20. The second part of verse 13 gives us a glimpse of another hopeful picture. What is the picture, and what do you think it might mean? Who is the "holy seed"? (See also Isaiah 11:1; we will study more about this picture later.)

Isaiah's barrier to freedom was demolished as the angel brought a message that went something like this: "You're free, Isaiah! Your sin is gone! You're clean and ready to be used by God!" Like Isaiah, we all have faults. We may become convinced that those faults disqualify us from the Lord's service. But let me assure you of this: He can use any one of us—broken vessels that we are—for His service.
—Charles Swindoll (*The Swindoll Study Bible*, 813)

Celebrate the Only Perfect King

Are you frustrated by the state of affairs in the world today? Division, hatred, and anger rage, even among some believers. For a season, my anxiety levels skyrocketed when I watched the news or engaged in political conversations. I felt myself drowning in a quicksand of anxiety and hopelessness, and I knew God didn't want me caught in this frustrating bog. Finally, I asked myself, "Sue, where does your ultimate loyalty lie—in a national human leader or in King Jesus?" How would you answer that question?

Delving into Isaiah's beautiful descriptions of King Jesus changed my loyalties from an earthly leader to the only leader worthy of our trust. I pray working through these lessons will transform your loyalty too, as well as your stress levels.

Misplaced loyalty isn't new. In this lesson, Isaiah asked the king of his country where his ultimate loyalty lay, and the king's answer illustrated his lack of faith and intention to trust other world leaders rather than God. Isaiah 7, 8, and 9 provide the details, reveal wondrous prophecies about King Jesus, and help us live as his all-in, dedicated subjects. But these truths are buried treasure. Plodding through the maze of unfamiliar names, places, and political craziness in these three chapters may perplex, and possibly frustrate, even the most intrepid Bible students. I'll attempt to simplify and set the scenes so we can concentrate on the prophetic portions of the passages.

Memorize John 1:1–5, 14

In the beginning was the Word, and the Word was with God, and the Word was God. He was with God in the beginning. Through him all things were made; without him nothing was made that has been made. In him was life, and that life was the light of all mankind. The light shines in the darkness, and the darkness has not overcome it. . . .

The Word became flesh and made his dwelling among us. We have seen his glory, the glory of the one and only Son, who came from the Father, full of grace and truth.

THE POLITICS

 Read Isaiah 7:1–9.

The political scene was a mess—similar to the political chaos many nations are experiencing today. The great nation of Israel under Solomon had now split into two nations—Israel and Judah. Ahaz ruled the little nation of Judah, where Isaiah lived, but regardless of its size, Judah was important in God's plans because it was the "house of David" (7:13), and God said that the Messiah would be a descendant of King David. God had promised his hand would remain on Judah.

Israel and Judah are still warring with each other, as are other small nations in the area—Aram, Syria, Edom, and Philistia. Constant skirmishes erupt, but all six are terrified of the two domineering world powers—Assyria and Egypt. So the little-nation kings plot, maneuver, and manipulate one another, feigning alliances to protect themselves.

Judah's king Ahaz had just learned that the kings of Aram and Israel had formed an alliance against his country with plans to put an end to the Davidic dynasty, to "tear it apart" and place their own puppet king in Ahaz's place (7:6). As a result, Israel, Aram, and Judah planned to join forces against the two superpowers. King Ahaz and his people were "shaken, as the trees of the forest are shaken by the wind" by this news (7:2).

What isn't evident in the book of Isaiah is that Ahaz was already thinking about making an alliance with Assyria. Second Kings 16:7 tells us that he sent messengers to the king of Assyria, saying, "I am your servant and vassal. Come up and save me out of the hand of the king of Aram and of the king of Israel, who are attacking me." With these messengers, he sent silver and gold out of the temple as a gift, a giveaway of where he had already placed his trust.

ISAIAH'S INTERVENTION

In the midst of this political turmoil, the Lord called Isaiah to meet with King Ahaz at an important and vulnerable aqueduct, an above-ground structure that carried water the nation would need when under attack.

1. Why do you think God instructed Isaiah to bring along his son Shear-Jashub (7:3)? (As noted earlier, the name's pronunciation is Share-YA-shube and the meaning is "a remnant will return").

2. How did God advise Isaiah to counsel King Ahaz (7:4)?

[King Ahaz asking Assyria for help] was like a mouse sending for the cat to help him against two rats!
—Alfred Martin (*Isaiah*, 39)

DIGGING DEEPER

God always preserves a remnant of faithful followers even when the majority fall away. What do Ezra 9:5–9; Isaiah 11:10–12; Jeremiah 23:1–4; Zechariah 8:9–13; and Romans 11:1–7 reveal about this reality? What does the fact that the Lord always ensures that a remnant is preserved tell you about him?

3. What covenant promises had God made to Judah, the house of David, in the past (2 Samuel 7:16; 1 Kings 8:22–25)? Why didn't king Ahaz need to fear that other nations might take over his country? However, what was the stipulation?

4. What else did Isaiah relate to Ahaz as a message straight from God (7:7)?

5. In verses 8–9a, God lists the kings and future kings of the two countries who have formed an alliance against Judah. What do you think God is communicating to Ahaz, and why does he emphasize the word "only"?

6. In verse 9b, God reveals to King Ahaz where his true protection comes from and what will happen if he doesn't turn back to trusting in God instead of his own political power and alliances with foreign nations. What does God say? How might these words apply to Christians and the way they view their earthly citizenship in individual nations today?

7. How might these words apply to you today as you consider where to place your trust and loyalty for ultimate security, safety, and protection? (Consider also Isaiah 8:11–13 and 1 Peter 3:14–16.)

May the God of hope fill you with all joy and peace as you trust in him, so that you may overflow with hope by the power of the Holy Spirit.
—Romans 15:13

DIGGING DEEPER

Read and reflect on Psalm 2. What do you learn about the "kings of the earth" who oppose God and plot against his ways? What is their ultimate end? Where do the wise place their trust? Why?

In this amazing interchange the holy God stoops to Ahaz's weakness and offers his weak faith the advantage of a sign, anything as deep or high as he could possibly think of. Isn't it amazing how patient God is in dealing with sinners like us? In effect he was handing Ahaz a blank check, asking him to fill in any amount!
—Andrew Davis (*Christ-Centered Exposition*, 49)

DIGGING DEEPER

Investigate how God uses signs in Gideon's life and ministry in Judges 6–7. How is this interchange with God different from that of Ahaz? What are the takeaways for us today?

DIGGING DEEPER

When does God prohibit us from demanding proof by asking for a sign, and when does he delight in showing us a sign? Compare Psalm 95:8–11 and Matthew 16:1–4 with 2 Kings 20:8–11 and Malachi 3:10.

GOD'S GRACIOUS SIGN

❋ Read Isaiah 7:10–17.

8. Through Isaiah, the Lord made an offer to Ahaz. What lengths was God willing to go to in order to move King Ahaz back to a stronger faith (7:10–11)?

9. How did Ahaz respond to God's offer (7:12)? Why do you think he refused to ask God for a sign?

10. How did Isaiah respond to Ahaz's reply (7:13)? How does Isaiah address King Ahaz, and what is he implying? What does this response tell you about Ahaz's heart toward God and his plans for the future?

God gives King Ahaz a sign whether he wants one or not:

> Therefore the Lord himself will give you a sign: The virgin will conceive and give birth to a son, and will call him Immanuel. (7:14)

This prophetic sign, like some others through the ages, had a double meaning. In one sense it related to the current situation, but in another sense it contained a future meaning. It's helpful to understand that the Hebrew word "almah" has two meanings—it can mean *virgin*, but also it can mean *young woman*. The prophecy relating to the current event meant that in Ahaz's time, a child would be born in the natural way and would be named "Immanuel," meaning *God with us*. This child served as a timetable for the fulfillment of a prophecy that related directly to King Ahaz's and Judah's circumstances.

11. What will occur by the time this normal boy reaches the age of accountability (7:15–16)?

12. What else will occur as a result of King Ahaz's lack of faith in God's promises to protect him and Judah from harm (7:17)? (Note: "Ephraim" is another name for "Israel.")

13. Who will orchestrate this future discipline (7:17)? Any thoughts as to why? What does this teach us about God's love for his people? Why does God discipline his beloved children (Hebrews 12:7–13)?

DIGGING DEEPER

Compare the pronouns in 7:11 and 13 in reference to God. What do you think this change indicates?

The prophet had called Yahweh "Ahaz's God" . . . , but now that the king had rebelled against Him, Isaiah referred to the Lord as "my (Isaiah's) God." This change was ominous, suggesting that God would abandon the king. If Ahaz's decision resulted in God withdrawing support from the Davidic kings, the prophecy of Immanuel may imply that God would raise up His own King from David's house who would be faithful to Him. This could explain why God gave such a major messianic prediction at this time.
—Thomas Constable
(*Notes on Isaiah*, 73)

14. Isaiah's prophecy in 7:14 also contained a grand future meaning that would bring the ultimate end to all chaos and turmoil in the world. Read Matthew 1:21–23. What does Matthew reveal about the future meaning of the prophecy in Isaiah 7:14? Who is this child?

15. What is unique about this child (Matthew 1:18)? Do you believe in the virgin birth of the Messiah? Why or why not?

After his disappointing encounter with King Ahaz at the aqueduct, Isaiah prophesizes details of Assyria's devastating sweep of these tiny nations, including Judah. They will be carried into humiliating exile and slavery, leaving once prosperous Israel and Judah full of "briers and thorns" (7:24–25), a place of utter "darkness" (8:22). Then in chapter 9, Isaiah writes a beautiful word—"Nevertheless."

DIGGING DEEPER

Why do you think it's vital that the Messiah have a human mother and a divine Father? Research reasons the virgin birth is one of the foundational doctrines of orthodox Christian faith.

ISAIAH PROPHESIZES CONCERNING A GREAT LIGHT

 Read Isaiah 9:1–7.

Through the ages, people have yearned for their national governments to be fair, just, and righteous. Yet again and again those governments have disappointed. Why? Because they are all led by finite humans. Will our yearnings ever be realized? Isaiah answers our question in the affirmative. We find the answer in Isaiah 9:1–7, one of the most famous passages in the book.

He looks like anything but a king. . . . Majesty in the midst of the mundane. Holiness in the filth of sheep manure and sweat. Divinity entering the world on the floor of a stable, through the womb of a teenager and in the presence of a carpenter.
—Max Lucado (*God Came Near*, 23)

16. In 9:1–2 what did God promise the Jews who had been exiled as well as those who have loved God through the ages?

17. How did Jesus fulfill this prophecy in his early earthly ministry (Matthew 4:12–17)?

ISAIAH DESCRIBES BELIEVERS' REJOICING

18. How did peoples in many of the ancient biblical cultures express their joy (9:3–5)? (Midian's defeat refers to a time when Gideon and his men trusted the Lord and defeated the cruel Midianites in a fierce battle without any weapons, recorded in Judges 6–7.)

DIGGING DEEPER

Why do you think Isaiah, Matthew, and Jesus referred to "Galilee of the nations," also translated "Galilee of the Gentiles"? See also Luke 2:29–32. What was the hidden message in these words?

19. Why will God's people rejoice (9:6)? Describe this new King. How do you know this passage cannot be referring to an earthly king?

ISAIAH DESCRIBES YOUR KINGDOM HOME

20. Write out verse 7 in the space below, savoring every word.

Surely the nations are like a drop in a bucket; they are regarded as dust on the scales; he weighs the islands as though they were fine dust. . . . Before him all the nations are as nothing; they are regarded by him as worthless and less than nothing.
—Isaiah 40:15, 17

21. Describe Jesus's millennial kingdom and government (9:7). How long will his kingdom last?

If you belong to God's forever family, Isaiah is describing your forever home in verse 7. How does this kingdom compare with where you live now? How do you feel as you anticipate living there forever? How does this realization influence how you live now?

22. Like King Ahaz, have you placed your faith more in human governments than in God? Why are human governments bound to fall short of our hopes and expectations for peace, righteousness, and justice? What has this lesson taught you?

Rejoice in Your Just King

Our family loves trees. One reason we purchased our present home is the abundance of huge trees not only in our yard but along the canal that runs parallel and down the hill from our backyard fence. Sweet gums, red oaks, and live oaks attract birds constantly singing, flitting, and bickering with pesky squirrels over who gets first dibs at the feeder. Right now, from my upstairs office window, as I write this study, I'm watching the wind rocking the trees' branches like a lullaby. There's just something life-giving about trees.

Soon after we moved in, and to our dismay, we realized that the roots of a majestic thirty-foot cottonwood tree were encroaching on our foundation, requiring a team of lumberjacks to saw it down. However, that tree refused to die. Although the tree had lost its grandeur and was now just a humble stump, hardy little saplings continued to sprout.

Like that stump, Israel and Judah, once flourishing nations, would soon endure seventy years of captivity in Babylon and Assyria. But a remnant of faithful Jews would return to their dried-up wasteland, and one day, out of that remnant, would come the Messiah, first as a humble "shoot" (11:1) and later as a mighty King.

THE STUMP AND SHOOT OF JESSE

 Read Isaiah 11:1.

1. Who was Jesse (Ruth 4:22)?

OPTIONAL

Memorize Colossians 1:15–17

The Son is the image of the invisible God, the firstborn over all creation. For in him all things were created: things in heaven and on earth, visible and invisible, whether thrones or powers or rulers or authorities; all things have been created through him and for him. He is before all things, and in him all things hold together.

2. The stump in 11:1 represents Jesse's genealogical lineage or family tree. What would grow out of the stump of his family tree, and what would it produce? What do you think Isaiah wanted to communicate using these analogies?

3. What promise did God make to Jesse's son (2 Samuel 7:16)? Why would this promise be an encouragement to the people of Judah at that time and to us today?

4. Who is this shoot and branch (Luke 1:29–33; 2:40)?

5. How do the following passages illustrate his humble beginnings and lifestyle?

    Luke 2:6–7

    Luke 2:22–24; Leviticus 12:8

Matthew 13:53–56

Matthew 8:20; 10:9–14

Matthew 27:57–60

6. He could easily have entered into the world as the son of a king or other high-ranking, wealthy noble. Why do you think he chose to be born into the poor family of a carpenter and live and minister among the common people?

DIGGING DEEPER

Read and contemplate Mary's song in Luke 1:46–55. What does her song tell us about her place in society, her humility, and her faith in God?

DIGGING DEEPER

What does the author of Hebrews say about why Jesus took on human form and dwelt among us (Hebrews 2:5–18)?

DIGGING DEEPER

God manifests himself as three persons, equal in essence but each serving a different function. The theological term for these three is the Trinity. They greet the seven churches in Revelation 1:4–8. Distinguish each person of the Trinity and how they are described. What truths can you glean concerning the work of the Trinity now and in eternity?

7. What difference does it make to you personally that Jesus came initially as a commoner rather than a king (Hebrews 2:17–18)?

YOUR JUST KING

 Read Isaiah 11:2–5.

8. Isaiah proclaims that the Holy Spirit will rest on the shoot of Jesse—Jesus, the Christ and Messiah (11:2). What qualities will King Jesus possess as a result (11:2–3)?

Note: The phrase "fear of the Lord" doesn't refer to terror or fright but to a holy reverence and respect, which the Son shows for the other members of the Trinity—the Father and the Spirit. They also show a similar respect and reverence for him, creating a beautiful unity in both essence and function.

9. In 11:3–5, what phrases inform us that these verses describe King Jesus when he returns to set up his millennial kingdom on the earth?

10. Have you ever felt frustrated by judicial systems overseen by finite human judges? How will King Jesus judge? Why will he be the first and only perfect judge? (11:3–4a)

11. God never guaranteed us that life in this fallen world would be just. Nevertheless, as Christians, how does God want us to interact with others (Micah 6:8)?

12. If all believers consistently lived out Micah 6:8, how do you think Jesus's reputation would be affected?

13. What can you do to better follow this mandate in your life today?

The twentieth century saw an experiment in governmentally forced sharing for the supposed benefit of the poor, called communism, and it has proven a gross economic, social, and moral failure all over the world. Representative democracy, with all its weaknesses and corruptions, still remains the best the human race has developed; but as Winston Churchill said famously, "Democracy is the worst form of government, except for all those other forms that have been tried from time to time."
—Andrew Davis (*Christ-Centered Exposition*, 574)

14. What will King Jesus do that will show he has authority over all the earth (11:4b)?

15. What's one reason living in King Jesus's millennial kingdom will be reason for exuberant celebration (11:5; Amos 5:24)?

In the messianic kingdom the martyrs will reclaim the world as the possession which was denied to them by their persecutors. In the creation in which they endured servitude, they will eventually reign.
—Church Father Irenaeus
(Quoted in *Heaven*, 52)

THE GREAT GATHERING TO KING JESUS

 Read Isaiah 11:10–12; 12:1–5.

16. What does Isaiah call King Jesus in 11:10? What might this name signify compared to calling him a shoot or a branch?

The title "Root of Jesse" presents the Messiah as the source of the Davidic line (cf. Genesis 3:15; 17:6), not just the product of that line.
—Thomas Constable
(*Notes on Isaiah*, 103)

17. What happens on that special day when King Jesus stands holding his banner (or a large flag) in 11:10–12?

18. In Isaiah 56:6–8, Isaiah makes a special point of informing us concerning who is included in that great gathering. A foreigner is anyone not of Jewish descent. How do you feel as you read this passage?

19. What excites you most about your eternal life with King Jesus? How might some of these realizations impact your priorities now?

DIGGING DEEPER

Study Luke 4:14–30. Why did the people in Jesus's hometown praise him at first and then try to throw him off a cliff later?

Pictures of Your Glorious Kingdom Home

History is dominated by the building of one vicious kingdom after another, all erected for the glory of sinful men who used conquest to etch their names in bloody monuments of their ambition. . . . But one day a gentle Jewish carpenter stood on trial before the most powerful empire on earth and proclaimed a different kind of kingdom than the world had ever seen.
—Andrew M. Davis (*Christ-Centered Exposition*, 243–244)

When Pontius Pilate, the Roman governor of Judea who sentenced Jesus to be crucified, asked Jesus if he was a king, Jesus replied in the affirmative but explained, "My kingdom is not of this world. If it were, my servants would fight to prevent my arrest by the Jewish leaders. But now my kingdom is from another place" (John 18:36).

The thought of living in a kingdom under the authority of a king probably feels strange to many of us. The *divine right of kings*—the belief that the kings derive their authority from God—is a form of government that passed the crown through royal family lines during Christendom's early centuries in the Western world. Depending on the character of each monarch, some kings and queens cared for their subjects with a measure of benevolence and kindness, while others enslaved them and used brutal tactics to control them. Americans fought a war to break away from the British monarchy and establish a representative form of government, hoping to create a form of checks and balances so that no one person could wield that much power over people again. But even different forms of republics and democracies have fallen short of the ideal.

As long as governments are led by flawed humans, they are bound to disappoint us. Our only hope of living in a place characterized by perfect peace, joy, security, and righteousness is to find a perfect person to govern us. We find that person in Jesus the Christ. He alone is worthy to be our King, and the Bible tells us that believers are actually destined to live in his kingdom.

The first time Jesus came to earth, he introduced us to a different kind of King—one who suffers to gain freedom for his people. At the conclusion of earth's history as we know it, Jesus will return to earth for a second time, but this time as a conquering King to set up a new kingdom on the earth. Faint glimpses of this kingdom are scattered throughout the Old and New Testaments, but we learn specifics in the final pages of Scripture. John, Jesus's beloved apostle, saw this kingdom and wrote down his vision in Revelation 20:1–6. Isaiah and other prophets fill in more details, but we'll start with a look at Revelation as a framework for the other prophecies about Jesus's coming kingdom.

JOHN'S VISION OF YOUR KINGDOM HOME

 Read Revelation 20:1–6.

1. How long does this passage say King Jesus's kingdom will last on the earth (20:6)?

2. What happens before Jesus sets up this kingdom (Revelation 20:1–2)? How will this change life on the earth?

What other important truth did God want John to reveal to us about King Jesus's millennial kingdom (Revelation 20:4)? What did Jesus tell us about this important truth (Matthew 16:27)? (We will learn more about our reigning with Christ and rewards in Jesus's kingdom in lesson 7.)

Revelation 20:5–6 refers to resurrections of both believers and nonbelievers.

- "The rest of the dead" probably refers to wicked people who died during the tribulation. They will not be resurrected until after Jesus's thousand-year kingdom reign. God will raise all the wicked from all eras at the same time. Learn more about the great white throne judgment in Revelation 20:11–15.

- "The first resurrection" in verse 6 refers to believers, who will be "priests of God and of Christ and will reign with him for a thousand years."

MILLENNIAL PEACE AND SAFETY

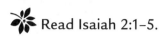 Read Isaiah 2:1–5.

3. The earth's landscape will be changed when King Jesus inaugurates his millennial kingdom on the earth. What is one aspect of that change (2:1–2)?

4. Who will teach us the Lord's ways, and how can we all live together in beauty, harmony, and righteousness (2:3)? What will this mean for your everyday life?

5. Describe how King Jesus's leadership will change people's lives and the interaction between nations (2:4). If King Jesus ruled the world today, how do you think news reporting and media would look different?

The Scriptures say very little about what we will do in heaven. But the Bible does say that Christians will reign with Christ in the administration of the millennial kingdom (Revelation 20:6). It also speaks of Christians reigning with Christ in eternity (Revelation 22:5)—in the new heavens and the new earth. Apparently Christians will be given spheres of authority in God's government both in the millennium and in the eternal state. These spheres of service will relate to how well we have served Christ in this life.
—John Walvoord
(*End Times*, 57)

Christians will never suffer injury or harm by the "second death." The second death is eternal separation from God. It follows the first death, which is separation of the soul from the body.
—Thomas Constable
(*Notes on Revelation*, 53)

In Heaven, the barriers between redeemed human beings and God will be gone forever. "The groanings and anguish which are general throughout creation" that Spurgeon speaks of will be replaced by the joy of seeing things clearly for the first time. Why? Because not only will we see God. He will be the lens through which we see everything else—people, ourselves, and the events of this life.
—Randy Alcorn (*We Shall See God*, 22)

 **Read Isaiah 11:6–9.**

6. Observe the ages of the various animals in verses 6–7. What does this reveal about the treatment of the weak and vulnerable in the kingdom?

7. How will the relationships between former hunters and their prey change?

8. How will parenting be affected?

9. What picture does Isaiah paint in the last part of 11:9? What do you think this means?

Read Isaiah 35:8–10.

10. Isaiah describes a particular highway in Jesus's millennial kingdom. What is it called? Who alone can travel on it? Where does it go? What is the mood as people travel?

A fuzzy hope in a brighter tomorrow might work for politicians trying to drum up support or poets hoping to tap sentimentality. Hope in Christ has therapeutic value because it is concrete. Specific promises. Particular expectations. Detailed descriptions. These facets present a painting that to our minds is more like a Rembrandt than a Monet.
—Michael Svigel (*Exploring Christian Theology*, 134)

11. How might traveling all over the new earth be affected by this new way of life in the millennial kingdom?

MILLENNIAL JUSTICE

 Read Zechariah 13:2.

12. What will happen to all forms of impurity in Jesus's millennial kingdom? How do you think this will influence the moral climate in the kingdom? What will this mean for your everyday life?

 Read Isaiah 24:21–23.

13. Who will finally reap the consequences of the pain and suffering inflicted on the earth? Describe the consequences they've brought upon themselves (24:21–22).

> Away with the noise of your songs! I will not listen to the music of your harps. But let justice roll on like a river, righteousness like a never-failing stream!
> —Amos 5:23–24

14. How does Isaiah describe King Jesus as he administers justice in the millennial kingdom (24:23)? How do you feel as you learn that ultimate justice is guaranteed?

 Read Isaiah 32:1–8.

15. What does verse 1 tell us about some Christians' roles in the kingdom?

16. How will these righteous rulers change the justice systems (32:2)? How will this change the moral climate in the kingdom? What does the fact that a justice system is needed tell you about the millennial kingdom?

17. How will noble and upright people be treated (32:3–4, 8)? How will fools and scoundrels be treated (32:5–7)? How will these changes affect the everyday lives of people who love the Lord?

MILLENNIAL JOY AND KNOWLEDGE OF GOD

 Read Isaiah 12:4–6.

18. How free will people be to proclaim God's story and glory? Who will have the opportunity to know the Lord personally and well, and to praise his beauty and righteousness? How will the world be different for everyone?

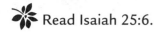 Read Isaiah 25:6.

19. What kinds of food and drink will we enjoy in the millennial kingdom? How do you feel as you read this verse?

For God did not appoint us to suffer wrath but to receive salvation through our Lord Jesus Christ. He died for us so that, whether we are awake or asleep, we may live together with him. Therefore encourage one another and build each other up, just as in fact you are doing.
—1 Thessalonians 5:9–11

MILLENNIAL HEALTH

 Read Isaiah 25:7–8 and 35:4–6.

20. What great fear will be erased for God's people in the millennial kingdom (25:7–8)?

DIGGING DEEPER

Describe our resurrected bodies from what we observe about Jesus's resurrected body (Luke 24:30–31, 36–43).

21. What is the promise to the blind, deaf, and lame under King Jesus's millennial rule (35:4–6)? How do you think the health of all people will be affected? Have you or a loved one struggled with any type of disability or infirmity? If so, how will your life be different in the millennial kingdom?

Read Isaiah 60:10–22.

DIGGING DEEPER

What can you learn about our new resur-rected bodies from 1 Corinthians 15:35–57?

22. What material goods will adorn the millennial kingdom? What else will make it a delightful place to live?

DIGGING DEEPER

Will the redeemed Jewish people be part of King Jesus's millennial king-dom? What promises does God make to them in Jeremiah 31:1–40?

23. Summarize what these passages tell us about what life will be like for believers in King Jesus's millennial kingdom. Envision living there. How might discovering these truths offer you courage for today?

Your Mighty King Rules with Compassion

D o you ever feel you are about to burst with good news? The promotion you've worked so hard to achieve. A loved one on the brink of death surprises everyone and revives. Finally the test is positive—or negative. You can't wait to shout it from the rooftops!

Isaiah had spent most of his ministry years shouting from the Jerusalem rooftops to deaf ears. Poor Isaiah! But God also had a positive purpose for Isaiah's ministry. God knew that during and after the Jews' humbling seventy years in exile, those who turned back to God, the faithful remnant, would desperately need the words of comfort and encouragement in Isaiah 40. We continue to need words of comfort and encouragement too.

I love Isaiah 40—in my estimation, it's one of the most splendid passages of divine literature. This chapter contains many of the essential truths of our faith, woven together like a master quilt or painting. As you savor the words, ask God to move these magnificent concepts from your head to your heart and then out to your hands as you prepare now for your new life in Christ, in King Jesus's millennial kingdom, and beyond into the new heavens and new earth that we'll learn about in lesson 7. And don't forget that who you become now and what you do in this life will have tremendous implications for your eternal life and who you bring with you.

VOICES CALLING

 Read Isaiah 40:1–11.

The first voice in Isaiah 40 is that of John the Baptist proclaiming that God is sending a Messiah in the future because God has compassion on all repentant people, including his beloved Jews. Jesus's sacrifice is retroactive and also the basis for the forgiveness of the sins of repentant Jews who had faith in God's promises in the Old Testament. The other voice is that of Isaiah, who is also prophesying of God's great plan to send a future Messiah (vv. 9–10).

OPTIONAL

Memorize Isaiah 43:1–3

Do not fear, for I have redeemed you; I have summoned you by name; you are mine. When you pass through the waters, I will be with you; and when you pass through the rivers, they will not sweep over you. When you walk through the fire, you will not be burned; the flames will not set you ablaze. For I am the LORD your God, the Holy One of Israel, your Savior.

1. As you read this text, underline every word that pertains to voices speaking or calling out. What do you observe?

2. Verses 1–2 are addressed to the Jewish people, and verse 2 uses past tense, as though their exile is over. What does God proclaim that should result in their great comfort (40:2)?

Receiving "double for all her sins" probably means that God has generously and graciously pardoned all her sins.

3. John the Baptist's voice is quoted in 40:3–5. What was his role in King Jesus's ministry? See Luke 3:1–6, 15–18, 21–23. Why do you think Isaiah includes this prophecy right after verses 1–2?

DIGGING DEEPER

Study John the Baptist's quote carefully in Isaiah 40:3–5. Why do you think he commanded that the terrain be changed, a custom to welcome an honored visiting king?

4. Although Jesus will not begin his earthly ministry for six hundred years, on what basis were the Jewish people's sins in the Old Testament forgiven (Genesis 15:6; Hebrews 11:8–11, 17–19)?

5. How do we know that Isaiah 40 isn't just for the Jews during Isaiah's time but also for New Testament believers (40:5)? Why is this passage great comfort for all people through the ages?

6. Another voice calls out, possibly to Isaiah, to shout out another message. What's the main point of the message in verses 6–8? What's the bad news? What's the good news?

We can never have too big a conception of God, and the more scientific knowledge (in whatever field) advances, the greater becomes our idea of His vast and complicated wisdom. Yet, unless we are to remain befogged and bewildered and give up all hope of ever knowing God as a Person, we have to accept His own planned focusing of Himself as a human being, Jesus Christ.
—J. B. Phillips (*Your God Is Too Small*, 120–121)

7. Who is commanded to shout out another message in verse 9? What's the good news (40:10)?

Reliance on the Word of God is not fatalistic or superstitious. It is not trust in something impersonal like the stars or a good-luck charm. It is trust in a person who committed to us and has all the resources necessary to care for us. . . . God's Word has the same character as God himself. It is unchanging and reliable as the God who speaks it.
—Barry Webb (*Message of Isaiah*, 163)

8. How is King Jesus described in verse 11? What words stand out to you? How might anyone who cares for young people be encouraged by this text? How would you apply this passage personally?

9. What essential truths of our faith are prophesied in Isaiah 40:1–11?

DIGGING DEEPER

Contrast the pictures of
King Jesus in 40:10–11.
What can you glean
from these very dif-
ferent portraits?

Come to me, all you who
are weary and burdened,
and I will give you rest . . .
for I am gentle and humble
in heart, and you will
find rest for your souls.
                —Matthew 11:28–29

DIGGING DEEPER

Study and meditate on
John 10:1–18, the Good
Shepherd. How does the
New Testament passage
complement your study of
the Shepherd in Isaiah 40?

This [40:12] is meant to
humble the arrogance of
humanity and put us in our
place. God is so immense
that he has measured the
waters of the seven seas in
his cupped hand, a stagger-
ing achievement because
the ocean—more than
six miles deep in places—
dwarfs the tiny stature of
a human being. If a person
tried to scoop out even a
bathtub full of water, it
would probably take more
than one thousand hand-
fuls to empty the tub!
        —Andrew Davis (*Christ-
        Centered Exposition*, 231)

Who alone is able to sovereignly reign over earth, her inhabitants, and her history? Who alone is able to redeem fallen mankind and accomplish the marvelous truths proclaimed in 40:1–13? Only the One described in verse 9: "Here is your God!" In the remaining sections of this chapter, Isaiah paints a breathtaking portrait of Almighty God. He alone is your eternal and righteous King, worthy of your focused worship and total loyalty. Savor his majesty.

HE IS SUPREME OVER CREATION

 Read Isaiah 40:12.

10. Isaiah asks us four questions. What is he describing? What is the answer to his questions?

11. What do you think Isaiah wants us to understand? Why?

HE KNOWS ALL THINGS

 Read Isaiah 40:13–14.

12. Isaiah asks four more questions. What are these questions about? What is the answer?

13. What do you think Isaiah wants us to understand? Why?

HE RULES OVER THE NATIONS

 Read Isaiah 40:15–17, 21–24.

14. How does Isaiah describe the value of all nations and their human leaders compared to God (40:15–17)?

DIGGING DEEPER

The book of Job ends with a series of similar questions. Read Job 38:1–42:6. After Job lost everything, he struggled to understand why God had allowed him to suffer so greatly. What was God teaching Job in these final chapters? Relate these findings to what Isaiah attempts to teach us in chapter 40.

15. How big is God according to verse 22? How do the earth and its inhabitants look to him?

The term "islands" can also be translated as "coastlands" and generally refers to all landmasses.

DIGGING DEEPER

Contrast the first questions of verse 12 with the first phrase of verse 15. What do you think Isaiah wants you to grasp?

16. What is God able to do to human rulers who seem all powerful in the eyes of those they govern (40:24)?

17. How might verse 24 apply to you today as you consider where to place your trust and loyalty for ultimate security, safety, and protection?

Idolatry isn't just one of many sins; rather it's the one great sin that all others come from. So if you start scratching at whatever struggle you're dealing with, eventually you'll find that underneath it is a false god. Until that god is dethroned, and the Lord God takes his rightful place, you will not have victory.
—Kyle Idleman (*Gods at War*, 22)

HE IS THE ONE TRUE GOD

 Read Isaiah 40:18–20.

Regardless of the obvious grandeur of Almighty God, prideful people have insisted on worshipping cheap substitutes for God.

18. What did wealthy people in many ancient civilizations do to replace God (40:18–19)? What did many poor people do (40:20)? Why were all their efforts so foolish?

19. We don't worship the kinds of idols that artists crafted in the ancient world. Nevertheless, we can easily make idols out of people and things today instead of God. Specifically, what idols often take God's place in societies today?

20. What kinds of idols are you tempted to worship? Can you discern why? What needs might you be attempting to meet by worshipping an idol instead of the one true God? Why is idol worship so futile?

HE CONTROLS THE HEAVENS

 Read Isaiah 40:25–26.

21. How do you feel when you look up into the vast heavens on a clear night? Who controls all those planets and stars, all that comprises the entire universe? What does this reality reveal about God?

HE STRENGTHENS THOSE WHO HOPE IN HIM

 Read Isaiah 40:27–31.

22. What complaint do Isaiah's people and people today sometimes make against God (40:27)? Have you ever made a similar complaint? What made you feel this way?

23. In contrast, what does God reveal about himself in verse 28?

24. What does our King do with his strength (40:29)?

The core problem isn't the fact that we're lukewarm, halfhearted, or stagnant Christians. The crux of it all is why we are this way and it is because we have an inaccurate view of God. We see Him as a benevolent Being who is satisfied when people manage to fit Him into their lives in some small way.
—Francis Chan
(*Crazy Love*, 22)

DIGGING DEEPER

Describe the competition between the Philistines' god Dagon and the Ark of the Covenant that held the presence of God in 1 Samuel 5:1–5. Who won? Why?

The God with whom we have to do is not a mere cosmic principle, impersonal and indifferent, but a living Person, thinking, feeling, active, approving of good, disapproving of evil, and interested in His creatures all the time.
—J. I. Packer (*Knowing God*, 74)

25. What does our God know about our lives in this fallen world (40:30)?

26. How does our King respond (40:31)?

DIGGING DEEPER

In verse 31, Isaiah says that when we hope in the Lord, we will soar like eagles. Investigate the flight of eagles to learn more about this analogy.

27. How much can you relate to the tired and weary, those in need of strength to run, or even just to walk and not stumble or faint? What have you learned about God in this chapter that might help you or someone you love regain vitality to press on?

The King's Servant Songs

What does "the cross" mean to you? It rests on the timeline of history like a compelling diamond. Its tragedy summons all sufferers. Its absurdity attracts all cynics. Its hope lures all searchers. . . . The cross is what counts. . . . A crucified carpenter claiming he is God on earth? Divine? Eternal? The death slayer? No wonder Paul called it "the core of the gospel." Its bottom line is sobering: if the account is true, it is history's hinge. Period. If not, it is history's hoax.
—Max Lucado (*No Wonder They Call Him Savior*, 13–14)

OPTIONAL

**Memorize
Romans 3:21–25**

But now apart from the law the righteousness of God has been made known, to which the Law and the Prophets testify. This righteousness is given through faith in Jesus Christ to all who believe. There is no difference between Jew and Gentile, for all have sinned and fall short of the glory of God, and all are justified freely by his grace through the redemption that came by Christ Jesus. God presented Christ as a sacrifice of atonement, through the shedding of his blood—to be received by faith.

Seven hundred years before Jesus's earthly ministry, Isaiah described Jesus as the Suffering Servant and provided details of that cross—Jesus's trial, abuse, crucifixion, burial, and resurrection, with related emotions of anguish and joy. In this lesson we'll concentrate on these breathtaking passages known as the four servant songs. Join me in the fascinating explorations of the millennial kingdom as it relates to Isaiah's prophecies concerning Jesus's first coming—when he took on a human body, took up residence with us here on earth, and voluntarily offered himself in our place on the cross so we might become daughters of the king and live forever in his kingdom.

THE FIRST SERVANT SONG

 Read Isaiah 42:1–9.

God the Father is speaking in these four verses.

1. Who will join the Father and the Son in implementing the historic events that redeem mankind, making Jesus's millennial kingdom and the new heavens and the new earth possible (42:1)?

In the past God spoke to our ancestors through the prophets at many times and in various ways, but in these last days he has spoken to us by his Son, whom he appointed heir of all things, and through whom he made the universe. The Son is the radiance of God's glory and the exact representation of his being, sustaining all things by his powerful word. After he had provided purification for sins, he sat down at the right hand of the Majesty in heaven.
—Hebrews 1:1–3

2. What will be one brand-new characteristic of Jesus's millennial kingdom (42:1)?

3. What do verses 3–5 reveal about the servant's character? In his first coming, his previous earthly ministry, how was he different from other kings?

The servant will undo all the horrendous and degrading effects that sin has had on the human race and restore to people their true freedom and dignity as sons and daughters of God.
—Barry Webb (*Message of Isaiah*, 172)

Now God speaks directly to the servant.

4. How involved is God the Father in the servant Son's ministry? How broad will their ministry be? (42:5–6)

5. What important tasks will the servant Son accomplish (42:7)?

6. How does God call Christians to imitate the Suffering Servant today in the passages below?

1 Peter 2:11–12

1 Peter 2:13–17

1 Peter 3:8–9

7. Although the words in verses 42:6–7 were spoken directly from God the Father to Jesus, his suffering-servant Son, we are called to follow in Jesus's footsteps and live the way he did. Specifically, how can you imitate the Suffering Servant in your personal life right now? What changes would you need to make to live this way?

8. What does God the Father say about himself and his plan in the announcement in 42:8–9?

DIGGING DEEPER

In the Gospels, compare and contrast examples of Jesus carrying out the tasks mentioned in 42:7.

 Read Isaiah 49:1–7.

In this song, we are privileged to eavesdrop on a conversation between God the Father and the servant Son.

9. In the first four verses, the servant Son speaks to the distant nations identifying the first people group he came to redeem. Who are these people (49:3–5)?

DIGGING DEEPER

Is the people group identified in 49:3 and 5 still high priority to the Trinity? Study Romans 11 to understand the heart of God for these people even today.

10. What does verse 4 reveal about his relationship with these people during Isaiah's lifetime?

11. What does God the Father say to the servant Son in verses 5–6? What difference does this announcement make to all peoples for all time?

He was chosen before the creation of the world, but was revealed in these last times for your sake. Through him you believe in God, who raised him from the dead and glorified him, and so your faith and hope are in God.
—1 Peter 1:20–21

12. According to verse 7, how do earthly governments treat the servant Son differently when he returns the second time?

THE THIRD SERVANT SONG

❊ Read Isaiah 50:4–7.

The incarnated servant Son, Jesus, was fully God and fully man in one person. In his humanity, Jesus felt temptation as we do, but he never sinned. Also, he prayed, asking God the Father for help and strength in his humanity, as he lived out his perfect life on earth as a model for us.

In these verses, we gain a glimpse into the beautiful partnership between God the Father and the servant Son during his earthly ministry.

13. How did God the Father help the servant Son in verse 4? How have you benefited from words Jesus spoke while here on earth in the first century? What specific passages have been the most meaningful in your life? What difference does it make in your life that Jesus is a skilled and caring listener?

14. What was the servant Son able to do with the Father's strength and help (50:5–6)? When did this abuse occur (Luke 22:63–65; 23:26–49)?

15. Because of the partnership of the Father and the Holy Spirit, what is the servant Son's attitude toward what he needs to do (50:7)? How might the imagery in this verse help you when you face a long-term trial?

Compare Philippians
2:1–11, also known as the
"kenosis" (the great empty-
ing), with Isaiah 52:13–14.

THE FOURTH SERVANT SONG—THE SUFFERING SERVANT

❊ Read Isaiah 52:13–15.

16. What does God the Father proclaim in these three verses? What do you learn about the servant Son's earthly ministry and his ultimate destiny (52:13–14)?

17. Who will change their minds about the Suffering Servant and why (52:15)?

❊ Read Isaiah 53:1–12.

Leviticus 16:14–15 uses the same word for "sprinkle" that Isaiah uses in 52:15. The Old Testament priests daily sprinkled the blood of sacrificed animals as atonement for the sin of the people. In contrast, the Suffering Servant's blood cleanses sinners from their sins once and for all.

18. What are the questions that begin this chapter (53:1)? Jesus's beloved disciple, John, refers to these questions in John 12:37–41. What do these verses reveal about those who believed and those who did not? What does verse 41 tell us about Isaiah 53?

He did not enter by means of the blood of goats and calves; but he entered the Most Holy Place once for all by his own blood, thus ob-taining eternal redemption.
—Hebrews 9:12

19. What do verses 2–3 disclose about Jesus's humanity? See also Isaiah 11:1 and 10.

20. Why did the servant suffer? What did his suffering accomplish? (53:4–5)

DIGGING DEEPER

Two other prophecies say that Christ was pierced—Zechariah 12:10 and Psalm 22:16. What insights can you draw from these prophecies?

21. Why do we all need forgiveness for sin (53:6)?

In 1947 a Bedouin shepherd boy named Muhammad climbed into a cave near Jericho and discovered the greatest archaeological find of the twentieth century: the Dead Sea Scrolls. The largest of them was the Isaiah scroll: carbon-14 dating sets its age at least as old as 230 BC—"*before Christ*," that is. Actually, the prophecy itself was originally made seven centuries before Jesus was born. And that makes Isaiah 53 a miracle!
— Andrew Davis (*Christ-Centered Exposition*, 317)

22. What was prophesied in 53:7? How do these New Testament verses fulfill this prophecy?

Matthew 27:14

John 1:29

1 Peter 2:21–25

23. What ultimately happened to the Suffering Servant (53:8; Romans 5:6–8; 2 Corinthians 5:21)? Why?

24. How was the prophecy in verse 9 fulfilled (Matthew 27:57–60)?

DIGGING DEEPER

How do you know that Isaiah 53 is about Jesus Christ and could never be fulfilled by any future Jewish leader, as some Jews argue today?

Let us run with perseverance the race marked out for us, fixing our eyes on Jesus, the pioneer and perfecter of faith. For the joy set before him he endured the cross, scorning its shame, and sat down at the right hand of the throne of God. Consider him who endured such opposition from sinners, so that you will not grow weary and lose heart.
—Hebrews 12:1–3

25. As a result of the great suffering of the servant, what is he promised (53:10–12)? How do you feel about the reality of Jesus's intense suffering on your behalf?

Your Kingdom Rewards

Early in Jesus's earthly mission, he returned to his hometown of Nazareth, where he was invited to speak as an honored guest in the synagogue (Luke 4:14–30). Rather than choose a text as preachers do today, customarily the rabbi stood and read the passage that came next in the scroll. Then he would sit down and explain it. The scroll just happened to be at Isaiah 61. Jesus read the opening words:

> The Spirit of the Sovereign LORD is on me, because the LORD
> has anointed me to proclaim good news to the poor. He has sent
> me to bind up the brokenhearted, to proclaim freedom for the
> captives and release from darkness for the prisoners, to proclaim
> the year of the LORD's favor.

He stopped reading in the middle of Isaiah 61:2. Then he rolled up the scroll, gave it back to the attendant, and sat down to explain it. He began with these words: "Today this scripture is fulfilled in your hearing." Everyone there knew that Jesus was proclaiming that he was the long-awaited Messiah—the Suffering Servant in Isaiah! Wouldn't you have loved to have heard the rest of his sermon?

But why did he stop in the middle of verse 2? Because the words he read pertained to his first advent, his first coming to earth as the Suffering Servant to atone for the sins of all who desired to be part of his forever family. The second part of verse 2 to the end of the passage pertains to his second advent, when he returns to earth as conquering king to set up his millennial kingdom, where those who love him will serve as his ministers and priests.

In this lesson we'll learn more about what our lives will be like in Jesus's future kingdom and beyond, our service in the kingdom, and how we can prepare for that service now.

OPTIONAL

**Memorize
Ephesians 6:7–8**
Serve wholeheartedly, as if you were serving the Lord, not people, because you know that the Lord will reward each one for whatever good they do.

The passage Jesus read was a messianic prophecy that envisioned a coming Messiah who would be both a servant to the needy and a king worthy of obedience and devotion. As one of Jesus's first statements regarding his earthly mission and identity as the Messiah, what he said at this small synagogue nestled along the shore of Galilee was a declaration to all who were in attendance that he had come for a specific and prescribed purpose.
—Michael Anthony ("The Heart of God and Social Engagement," *Bibliotheca Sacra*, 263)

 Read Isaiah 61:1–2a.

1. In what sense was Jesus's first mission on earth good news, or gospel, to the poor, the brokenhearted, and prisoners?

2. How did some Jewish leaders argue that they weren't like the people who needed what Jesus offered (John 8:31–36)?

3. Read Matthew 5:3–10 for more insight on the kinds of people Jesus came to redeem. What will they inherit (vv. 5 and 10)?

4. Do you see yourself as one of the people mentioned in Isaiah 61:1 or Matthew 5:3–10? If so, in what sense?

God is musing aloud [in Isaiah 66:1-2] about a suitable temple, a fitting place where He might rest. The answer is beautiful: He is at home with the person who has a humble, contrite spirit, who trembles at His Word, who reveres Him. A person with that kind of spirit is God's house. That is where He is at work.
—Charles Swindoll (*Swindoll Study Bible*, 869)

5. As you grow in your faith, how can you become more like people mentioned in Isaiah 61:1 and Matthew 5:3–10?

JESUS'S SECOND ADVENT

❋ Read Isaiah 61:2b–11.

DIGGING DEEPER

Study Revelation 19:11–21 for details of this fierce battle known as the battle of Armageddon.

The part of Isaiah 61:2 that Jesus did not read begins "and the day of vengeance of our God." When Jesus returns to earth a second time, he will come back as a conquering warrior to cleanse the earth of injustice and all the abuse committed through the ages, preparing the earth for his thousand-year kingdom.

6. How does his future return "comfort all who mourn, and provide for those who grieve" (61:2b–3)?

7. How will Jesus dress those who love him? What will each piece of adornment replace? (61:3)

For the Church has no beauty but what the Bride-groom gives her; he does not find, but makes her, lovely.
—C. S. Lewis (*The Four Loves*, 105)

8. Do you enjoy being well dressed? How will this new "outfit" make you feel?

Blessed and holy are those who share in the first resurrection. The second death has no power over them, but they will be priests of God and of Christ and will reign with him for a thousand years.
—Revelation 20:6

9. Isaiah uses a botanical analogy to describe Jesus's beloved at the end of verse 3. What is the analogy, and what does it communicate? What do you think of this new name?

10. What will be one of the service projects for believers in the millennial kingdom (61:4)?

11. Can you think of ruined cities or ancient ruins that are in need of restoration? How does verse 4 offer hope that one day these places will be redeemed and full of beauty and life?

12. Who will help believers restore the land to its pre-fall beauty and vitality (61:5)?

13. What will be the primary service of many believers in Jesus's millennial kingdom? Who will support your work and honor you for your service? (61:6). How can you prepare now so you will be ready for that future role?

Throughout the Old Testament the possession of the earth by the righteous is a common theme and refers to the rule of the saints in the future kingdom.
—Joseph Dillow (*Reign of the Servant Kings*, 77)

14. In ancient civilizations, the first son in the family received a double portion of his father's inheritance. How many believers are considered honored first sons in God's family, and what does it mean that each will receive a double portion (61:7)?

15. What does God hate, and why will he reward his people for the good they do during their time on the earth (61:8)? Do you share disdain for what he "hates" in yourself? In others? If so, how do you express those convictions while still loving yourself and other sinful people well?

16. Have you ever lived in a place where natural beauty flourishes? If so, that's just a foretaste of one of the rewards all believers will enjoy living in the millennial kingdom. Verses 9–11 describe that beauty. What analogies picture the changes of a post-fall earth to an Eden-like earth, where righteousness flourishes and Jesus reigns as King?

BELIEVERS' REWARDS REVEALED IN THE NEW TESTAMENT

Not only will you be living in a place that's far more naturally majestic than any spot on this fallen earth that you've ever vacationed or viewed in pictures, but you'll also receive individual rewards to enhance the joy of everyday life. Your rewards will be revealed at a future time and place that the Bible calls a "judgment" (2 Corinthians 5:10), but don't let this term frighten you. Believers' "judgment" will be a time of exuberant joy for most, although some may experience regret.

The Bible speaks of two different judgments, but as a believer you will only experience one of them:

- The great white throne judgment for nonbelievers (Revelation 20:11–15)
- The judgment seat of Christ, also known as the bema seat, for believers (2 Corinthians 5:9–10)

Since Isaiah 61 teaches us about believers' rewards, we'll focus on this second judgment. Remember that the assurance of our salvation is not in question. All Christians will spend eternity with the Lord. The judgment seat of Christ is the place where believers will receive various rewards, honors, and commending words from Jesus. In addition, believers will learn about the ministerial role they will each inherit, depending on what they have done or not done during their lifetime.

17. How do the following verses support the idea of believers inheriting rewards?

Matthew 5:5, 10, 12

Matthew 6:1, 4

Matthew 16:27

Luke 6:23, 35

Ephesians 6:8

Colossians 3:24

Hebrews 11:26

Revelation 22:12

 Read 2 Corinthians 5:9–10.

18. What is our goal as Christians (5:9)? What is one reason we are motivated to do this (5:10)?

DIGGING DEEPER

Jesus told two parables that seem to contradict each other—the parable of the workers in the vineyard (Matthew 20:1–16) and the parable of the ten minas (Luke 19:11–27). Compare the two parables and discern which teaches about assurance of salvation and which teaches about eternal rewards.

 Read 1 Corinthians 3:8–15.

19. Although we will be rewarded individually, how does Paul instruct us to view our service for Jesus (3:8–9)? Discuss whether or not you struggle with this and if so, why?

20. On what foundation has Paul built his service for Jesus (3:10–11; Ephesians 2:19–22)? In what sense must this also be our foundation for service for Jesus? Why?

Great and mighty God, whose name is the LORD Almighty, great are your purposes and mighty are your deeds. Your eyes are open to the ways of all mankind; you reward each person according to their conduct and as their deeds deserve.
—Jeremiah 32:18–19

21. Paul names six different materials we may use to build a life of good works (3:12). What are they? Imagine a building composed of these materials. How durable would they be? How resistant to destruction?

The "Day" that Paul talks about in verse 13 is the day we will each stand before the judgment seat of Christ, the bema, to receive rewards.

22. What will happen on that "Day" (3:13)?

23. Would Paul rather be judged by Jesus or by another human being (see 1 Corinthians 4:2–5)?

If your enemy is hungry, give him food to eat; if he is thirsty, give him water to drink. In doing this, you will heap burning coals on his head, and the LORD will reward you.
        —Proverbs 25:21-22

How about you? How might the following verses affect your choice?

Romans 8:1

Romans 8:31, 35–39

2 Corinthians 8:9

24. If your service for Jesus is worthwhile, what will you receive (1 Corinthians 3:14)? If it is not, what will happen (3:15)? What do you think this means? Does this reality concern you? Motivate you? Scare you?

25. As you evaluate your life, would you say your service has been composed of gold, silver, costly stones, wood, hay, or straw? As you contemplate the exciting life of service that awaits you in the millennial kingdom, how would you like to serve your King there? What would you like to change about your life right now to increase the likelihood that you'll be given that opportunity?

Behold the New Heavens and the New Earth

As Isaiah closes his book, he offers us a glimpse of the new heavens and the new earth. We'll begin there and then move to the last two chapters of Revelation, where we learn more details from the apostle John's vision of the new universe that follows Jesus's thousand-year kingdom on the earth.

In these passages, scholars argue over what is literal and what is figurative, what is exactly the way it will be and what is a symbol of something impossible for us to fully comprehend. Let's not argue over these questions. Let's simply agree that these words are inspired by Almighty God, that they are breathtaking and incredibly exciting. Let's agree that they give us hope and help us persevere in our fallen abode now, as we prepare for an eternity with our God.

Isaiah grants us a peek. John's vision is full of dynamic details mixed together: a brilliant city, an elegant wedding, walls of jasper, and giant pearl gates. Pictures of life abound: the book of life, the tree of life, pure life-giving water flowing from God's throne in waterfall cascades. All that is beautiful and blessed is there, twirling together in splendor and majesty, created as the place for us to worship and serve God for eternity.

Walk with me through Isaiah's final glimpses of eternity, then through John's vision of the city as we take in the highlights. Breathe in the sights and smells. Listen for the soothing sounds, and rejoice that you are the bride of the Lamb and this new universe will be your new permanent home.

OPTIONAL

Memorize
Revelation 21:3–4
And I heard a loud voice from the throne saying, "Look! God's dwelling place is now among the people, and he will dwell with them. They will be his people, and God himself will be with them and be their God. 'He will wipe every tear from their eyes. There will be no more death' or mourning or crying or pain, for the old order of things has passed away."

Therefore, what we see in the Scripture's vision of the end of redemptive history is not an earth thrown in the trash can with its righteous inhabitants escaping to disembodied bliss in the clouds but a restored earth where creation has been reconciled to God.
—Matt Chandler (*The Explicit Gospel*, Kindle)

You may be wondering what happens to believers who die before the "rapture," when Jesus snatches them from the earth. Where does he take them? The first-century Thessalonians asked the same question, and Paul gives us marvelous insights that are detailed in my study on 1 & 2 Thessalonians. In a nutshell, many scholars believe that:

- Christians who die before the rapture go into God's presence to await the rapture. (See the intro section on page 15–16 for details.)
- After the rapture they enjoy God's presence and are spared the horrible seven-year tribulation that will end fallen earth's history.
- After the tribulation they return with Christ and enter into his millennial kingdom that we've learned so much about in this study.

Several events occur during those seven years we spend with Jesus waiting for the tribulation to end on earth. They include the bema seat judgment for believers and the marriage feast of the Lamb. These events, and probably others not revealed, prepare us for reigning with Christ in the millennial kingdom. Yes, it's complicated, but God expects us to work the puzzle pieces he's provided in Scripture as incentives to live courageously today.

ISAIAH'S PREVIEW OF OUR NEW ETERNAL HOME

 Read Isaiah 65:17–25.

1. How will we think about the past once we live permanently in the new heavens and the new earth (65:17)? As a result, what does Paul advise in 2 Corinthians 4:16–18? How might taking Paul's advice seriously help you now?

2. This new heavens and new earth is only for God's people. What brings God great delight (65:18–19)?

Often God speaks to us in words we can understand based on our past experiences. Some scholars believe that's what God is doing in 65:20.

3. Name the experiences in verse 20 that have brought untold misery and weeping to people living in a fallen world. Have you ever experienced any of these tragedies? Does knowing that these kinds of miseries have an expiration date help you now? If so, how?

4. Will there be productive work in eternity (65:21–22)? What does that teach us about the value of work now and its benefits?

5. In verse 23 God says that no parent will deal with a child "doomed to misfortune." Have you dealt with this kind of situation? How do you feel about living for eternity where this kind of tragedy will never occur again?

DIGGING DEEPER

How does this new universe compare with the world God first created in Eden (Genesis 1–2)? What insights about the new heaven and earth can you glean from descriptions of Eden?

6. Describe our relationship with our God (65:24). How does this compare with Adam and Eve's relationship with God in the garden of Eden (Genesis 3:8)?

7. Not only will discord between people and nations disappear from the earth, but where else will harmony reign (65:25)?

JOHN'S VISION OF THE NEW UNIVERSE

 Read Revelation 21.

8. In your mind's eye, picture what John saw in 21:1–2. How has life as we know it changed? How final is this transformation? What are the four new names given to our new home?

9. What did God reveal to John about our eternal life in 21:3–4 and 7? How do you feel as you read these amazing promises?

ETERNAL MARRIAGE TO THE LAMB

10. Now one of the seven angels in Revelation whisks John off in another vision. What is the angel showing John in 21:9? What does this insinuate has occurred? See Revelation 19:6–9. What does this imply concerning our eternal state with God?

11. Next the angel shows us our new home (21:10). What details regarding its appearance does the angel supply (21:11–14)? What is significant about the two sets of names that are written on the gates and on the foundations?

12. When God created mankind, he placed us in a garden, but our future abode is in a city. This megacity defies any place we have ever known. It is as tall as it is wide, probably square in shape. Generally, what is your impression of this massive city (21:15–21)?

Picture the colors of the stones that make up the city—opaque jasper (usually a dark red) and others that sparkle like transparent crystal, including sapphire (blue or violet), emerald, agate (milky or gray), onyx (various colors), ruby, chrysolite (referring to either quartz or topaz, golden yellow), turquoise, beryl (blue-green or green), jacinth (blue), and amethyst.

CITY OF LIGHTS

13. Three things will be missing from this city. What are they, and why don't we need them (21:22–23)? What does the absence of celestial bodies imply about the new heavens and the atmosphere surrounding the new earth?

The overall impression of the city as a gigantic brilliant jewel compared to jasper, clear as crystal, indicates its great beauty. John was trying to describe what he saw and to relate it to what might be familiar to his readers. However, it is evident that his revelation transcends anything that can be experienced.
—John Walvoord and Roy Zuck (*Bible Knowledge Commentary*, 985)

14. In 21:24, John says that the "kings of the earth will bring their splendor into" the city. Who do you think are the kings of the earth? What is John insinuating by this statement?

15. Why is there no need to ever shut the gates of this massive holy city (21:25)? Why were city gates closed in the past? How does that make you feel?

In short, ancient kings served as the primary authorities over the broad patterns of the cultural lives of their nations. And when they stood over against other nations, they were the *bearers*, the *representatives*, of their respective cultures. To assemble kings together, then, was in an important sense to assemble their national cultures together. The king of a given nation could bear, singly, a far-reaching authority that is today divided among many different kinds of leaders: the captains of industry; the molders of public opinion in art, entertainment and sexuality; educational leaders; representatives of family interests; and so on. This is why Isaiah and John could link the entrance of the kings into the City with the gathering in of the "wealth of the nations."
—Richard Mouw
(*When the Kings Come Marching In*, 50)

DIGGING DEEPER

Compare John's vision in 21:1–4 with Isaiah's glimpses of the new universe (Isaiah 65:17–25) hundreds of years earlier. What do you learn about prophecy and God?

DIGGING DEEPER

What will end (22:3)? Compare life in the new universe with life in our fallen world. How did Genesis 3 and the effects of sin change Eden? How will God's creation of a new heavens and a new earth change relationships? Mental and physical health? Economy? Governments and nations? Agriculture?

THE CENTER OF THE CITY

 Read Revelation 22.

16. Describe what John saw in the middle of the great city (22:1–2). What do you think might be the significance of the water, trees, and fruit?

17. What will people who loved and followed God be doing in this majestic city (22:3–5)? See also 2 Timothy 2:12a and Revelation 5:9–10. What do you think this kind of ministry will entail?

18. Considering how God fashioned you with gifts, passions, and interests, how would you like to serve God for eternity? What do you think this might look like in the new universe? What will qualify people for these different ministries?

19. How does knowing you will use your gifts, passions, and interests forever encourage you to develop these areas of your life now? What priorities in your life need to change right now so that you invest more in eternity and less in the temporary?

FINAL WORDS FROM JESUS TO JOHN

20. What does Jesus proclaim in 22:7, 12, and 16?

21. The last commands in the Bible are found in 22:8–10. What happened, and what are the commands?

22. Jesus tells John in 22:7, 10 to write down and share what he has seen, heard, and learned. Why?

23. In what sense is our time near, regardless of how long we live on the earth? How much time do you think you have left in this life? How do you plan to spend it? Has this study changed your plans and if so, how?

Hundreds of prophecies have come to pass exactly as the Bible has said, which is absolute proof that the Bible is the inspired Word of the Sovereign Lord. According to prophecy scholar John Walvoord, the Bible contains about one thousand prophecies of which about five hundred have already been fulfilled. The Bible has an amazing track record of 100 percent accuracy 100 percent of the time. It is batting 1,000.
— Mark Hitchcock
(*The End*, 15)

DIGGING DEEPER

Compare the first two chapters of the Bible with the last two chapters. How many similarities can you find? What has God done throughout the earth's history on behalf of his beloved people and creation? How have you personally benefited?

24. We spend quite a bit of time in this life getting and keeping things clean, but that won't be needed in our glorious futures. In 22:14 Jesus blesses those who "wash their robes" with the right to live in the eternal city and enjoy eternal life with God. Have you washed your robes? If not, what is keeping you from entering into these marvelous blessings? Consider talking about your questions with a woman who loves and knows God.

25. The Spirit and the bride make a final plea in 22:17. What is the plea and what is the free gift?

26. What are the warnings in verses 18–19? What do you think this means? How serious is God about the way his Word is handled?

27. Jesus makes us a promise in 22:20. What is his promise? How do you feel about this truth?

Wait Well for Your King and His Kingdom

I hate to wait; yet waiting transforms us. God blesses us when he orchestrates a variety of situations that require us to wait, although few of us appreciate this "blessing." My academy of waiting began my first year in college. As an only child growing up without Christian instruction, I never learned to share. Everything in my bathroom was mine. My roommates abruptly awakened me to the reality that this was no longer true. I had to wait my turn.

God's advanced waiting curriculum really kicked in with the birth of my first child. Suddenly, endless days of waiting lay before me—waiting for my milk to come in, waiting for the pharmacy to open, waiting to find out if the doctor would insist we bottle feed due to a persistent infection, waiting for my baby to stop screaming while I'm waiting for water to heat up to warm the bottle, waiting until she could eat solid food, waiting for dad to come home to help, and I could go on and on.

What a contrast to the glory days in college of sitting through stimulating lectures, reading interesting books, attending fun parties and athletic events, enjoying outings with friends, and writing for the college newspaper! Yet if I were to measure which experience better prepared me to serve the Lord and love others well, I'd have to choose mothering.

God may orchestrate a completely different curriculum for you, but whatever it is, if you choose to wait well, God will use this to sculpt a Christlikeness in you. He will enlarge your heart and create in you a capacity for wisdom and joy despite challenges. You'll naturally bear the winsome fruit of love, kindness, and perseverance. You'll learn to invest in eternity and prepare well for service in Christ's millennial kingdom and in the new heavens and the new earth. And that's the ultimate long-term investment!

OPTIONAL

Memorize
Hebrews 9:27–28
Just as people are destined to die once, and after that to face judgment, so Christ was sacrificed once to take away the sins of many; and he will appear a second time, not to bear sin, but to bring salvation to those who are waiting for him.

WHAT ARE YOU WAITING FOR?

Through the centuries, millions of believers have joined us in anticipation of Jesus's second coming. Let's learn from the directives given to our first-century brothers and sisters who will inherit the kingdom with us.

 Read 1 Thessalonians 1:8–10.

1. The first-century Thessalonian believers invested in a strong church that waited well. What did they do while they waited (1:8–9)? How can you help your church receive the praise and rewards that the Thessalonians will receive at Jesus's judgment seat of rewards?

2. What specifically were the Thessalonians waiting for (1:10)? What have you learned in this study that helps you understand verse 10?

 Read Titus 2:11–14.

3. Who is the "grace" of God in verse 11?

4. What is "grace" specifically teaching us to do as we wait (2:12–13)? Which of these mandates is the most difficult for you? Why? What will help you live all in for King Jesus and his coming kingdom?

5. What were the people in Titus's churches in Crete waiting for (2:13)? What incentive did this provide for them and us to be "eager to do what is good"?

I waited patiently for the LORD; he turned to me and heard my cry. He lifted me out of the slimy pit, out of the mud and mire; he set my feet on a rock and gave me a firm place to stand. He put a new song in my mouth, a hymn of praise to our God. Many will see and fear the LORD and put their trust in him.
—Psalm 40:1–3

Read 1 John 2:28–3:3.

6. What incentive does John give us for living lives dedicated to Jesus now (2:28)? What "coming" is John talking about? How do you want to feel when you stand before Jesus on that day?

7. How can you be assured of great joy and rewards when you stand before Jesus at the judgment seat of Christ (2:29; 2 Peter 1:10–11)?

DIGGING DEEPER

Does 1 John 2:29 mean that we must always do "what is right" in order to inherit the blessings of the kingdom? What provisions has God given to help us deal with our sin (1 John 1:8; 5:11–12)? Nevertheless, what are the benefits of living all in for Jesus?

8. What does God call us? What does he lavish upon us? (3:1)

DIGGING DEEPER

What does Peter mean when he writes about confirming one's calling and election? Study 2 Peter 1:3–11. What will be involved in receiving "a rich welcome into the eternal kingdom of our Lord and Savior Jesus Christ" (1:11)?

9. What are the promises in verse 2? Imagine the scene that day. How can you prepare for that day now? What does John suggest (3:3)?

Do not rebuke an older man harshly, but exhort him as if he were your father. Treat younger men as brothers, older women as mothers, and younger women as sisters, with absolute purity.
—1 Timothy 5:1–2

❋ Read Romans 8:18–25.

10. While these verses were written to the church in Rome, these promises are for all believers. What did Paul say in verse 18 to encourage us to persevere in whatever circumstances we are enduring? What do we have to look forward to? When will that glory be revealed both for them and for believers today?

11. Besides believers, what waits eagerly for King Jesus to return (8:20–21)? Why? What do you think this means?

12. Imagine the whole earth returning to a garden-like place similar to Eden but also retaining the attributes of the most beautiful cities on earth. What benefits will we see in eternity that we enjoy now in both country and city living?

13. Several times in this text and in the 1 John passage, Paul and John refer to Christians as "children of God" (8:19, 21; 1 John 3:1). Why do you think they use this terminology?

14. What is one of the grand benefits of adoption and "sonship" according to 8:23 and 1 Corinthians 15:42–44?

DIGGING DEEPER

Why are women adopted and given the honor of "sonship" instead of "daughtership"? Research the first-century Roman customs related to the privileges of sons for answers.

15. How does Paul implore us to "wait" (Romans 8:24–25)? How can you apply that directive in your life today?

REFLECTING ON OUR JOURNEY

16. How has your study of the King Jesus and his future kingdom affected your view of Jesus Christ?

Yet the LORD longs to be gracious to you; therefore he will rise up to show you compassion. For the LORD is a God of justice. Blessed are all who wait for him!
—Isaiah 30:18

17. How has this study impacted the way you think about your future? Are you expectant? Fearful? Oscillating? Can you determine why?

18. What have you learned from others in your group? Can you recall particular insights that encouraged or challenged you? Has anyone inspired you in your walk with Christ? If so, why not tell them?

19. What decisive steps can you take now to ensure that you benefit from what you have learned as you prepare to make your new home in the millennial kingdom and the new heavens and the new earth?

20. How have the truths about King Jesus and his coming kingdom changed the way you think, act, and serve?

21. God included these concepts in his Word to give you assurance of his coming kingdom and to prepare you for your eternal home. Has he succeeded in his desire?

He who testifies to these things says, "Yes, I am coming soon."
Amen. Come, Lord Jesus.
—Revelation 22:20

Works Cited

Alcorn, Randy. *We Shall See God: Charles Spurgeon's Classic Devotional Thoughts on Heaven*. Carol Stream, IL: Tyndale House Publishers, 2011.

Anthony, Michael J. "The Heart of God and Social Engagement." *Bibliotheca Sacra*, 176, no. 703 (July–September 2019). Published by Dallas Theological Seminary.

Bisagno, John R. *God Is*. Wheaton, IL: Victor Books, 1983.

Chan, Francis. *Crazy Love: Overwhelmed by a Relentless God*. With Danae Yankoski. Colorado Springs, CO: David C. Cook, 2008.

Chandler, Matt. *The Explicit Gospel*. With Jared C. Wilson. Wheaton, IL: Crossway, 2012.

Constable, Thomas L. *Notes on Isaiah*. Sonic Light. 2020 edition. 2021 edition found here: https://planobiblechapel.org/tcon/notes/pdf/isaiah.pdf.

————. *Notes on Revelation*. 2021 edition. https://planobiblechapel.org/tcon/notes/pdf/revelation.pdf.

Davis, Andrew M. *Christ-Centered Exposition: Exalting Jesus in Isaiah*. Nashville, TN: B & H Publishing Group, 2017.

Dillow, Joseph C. *The Reign of the Servant Kings: A Study of Eternal Security and the Final Significance of Man*. Hayesville, NC: Schoettle Publishing Co., 1992.

Edwards, Jonathan. "The Christian Pilgrim." SermonIndex.net, 1733 (original date of publication). Accessed Feb. 22, 2022. https://www.sermonindex.net/modules/articles/index.php?view=article&aid=3416.

Hendricks, Howard G., and William D. Hendricks. *Living by the Book: The Art and Science of Reading the Bible*. Chicago, IL: Moody Publishers, 2007.

Hitchcock, Mark. *The End: A Complete Overview of Bible Prophecy and the End of Days*. Carol Stream, IL: Tyndale House Publishers, 2012.

Idleman, Kyle. *Gods at War: Defeating the Idols That Battle for Your Heart*. Grand Rapids, MI: Zondervan, 2013.

Irenaeus. Quoted in *Heaven: A History* by Colleen McDannell and Bernhard Lang. New Haven, CT: Yale University Press, 1988.

Jensen, Irving L. *Isaiah & Jeremiah: A Self-Study Guide*. Chicago, IL: Moody Press, 1968.

Lewis, C. S. *The Four Loves*. Boston, MA: Houghton Mifflin Harcourt, 2011. Kindle.

Lucado, Max. *God Came Near: Chronicles of the Christ*. Colorado Springs, CO: Multnomah Press, 1987.

_____. *No Wonder They Call Him Savior: Chronicles of the Cross*. Portland, OR: Multnomah Press, 1986.

Lutzer, Erwin W. *Your Eternal Reward: Triumph and Tears at the Judgment Seat of Christ*. Chicago, IL: Moody Publishers, 1998.

Martin, Alfred. *Isaiah: The Salvation of Jehovah*. Moody Colportage Library series. Chicago, IL: Moody Press, 1956.

McClain, Alva J. Chapter 18, "The Blessings of the Prophetic Kingdom." *The Greatness of the Kingdom*. Chicago, IL: Moody Press, 1968.

Mouw, Richard J. *When the Kings Come Marching In: Isaiah and the New Jerusalem*. Revised ed. Grand Rapids, MI: Wm. B. Eerdmans Publishing Co, 2002.

Ortlund, Raymond C., Jr. *Isaiah: God Saves Sinners*. Preaching the Word series. Wheaton, IL: Crossway Books, 2005.

Packer, J. I. *Knowing God*. Downers Grove, IL: InterVarsity Press, 1973.

Phillips, J. B. *Your God Is Too Small: A Guide for Believers and Skeptics Alike*. New York, NY: Simon & Schuster, 2004.

Richard of St. Victor. Quoted in *Delighting in the Trinity: An Introduction to the Christian Faith*, by Michael Reeves. Downers Grove, IL: IVP Academic, 2012.

Spurgeon, Charles. Sermon no. 2211, "God Rejoicing in the New Creation." Spurgeongems.org. Accessed February 26, 2022. https://www.spurgeongems.org/sermon/chs2211.pdf.

Stott, John R. W. *Revelation: The Triumph of Christ*. With Dale and Sandy Larsen. Downers Grove, IL: InterVarsity Press, 2008.

Strauss, Richard L. *The Joy of Knowing God*. Neptune, NJ: Loizeaux Brothers, 1984.

Svigel, Michael J. *Exploring Christian Theology: The Church, Spiritual Growth, and the End Times*. Minneapolis, MN: Bethany House Publishers, 2014.

Swindoll, Charles. *The Swindoll Study Bible: Trusted Wisdom, Practical Application, Refreshing Insight, New Living Translation*. Carol Stream, IL: Tyndale House Publishers, 2017.

Tomba, Neil. Multiple "Jesus the King" sermons in 2020 and 2021. Northwest Bible Church. Accessed Feb. 22, 2022. northwestbible.org/sermon-series/jesus-the-king.

Walvoord, John F. *End Times: Understanding Today's World Events in Biblical Prophecy*. Swindoll Leadership Library series. Nashville, TN: Word Publishing, 1998.

Walvoord, John F., and Roy B. Zuck, eds. *The Bible Knowledge Commentary: An Exposition of the Scriptures*. Colorado Springs, CO: David C. Cook, 1983.

Webb, Barry G. *The Message of Isaiah: On Eagles' Wings*. The Bible Speaks Today series, edited by J. A. Motyer. Downers Grove, IL: InterVarsity Press, 1996.

About the Author

Sue Edwards is professor of educational ministries and leadership (her specialization is women's studies) at Dallas Theological Seminary (DTS), where she has equipped men and women for future ministry for over twenty years. Before teaching in the academy, she ministered as a Bible teacher, curriculum writer, and overseer of several megachurch women's ministries. As minister to women at Irving Bible Church and director of women's ministry at Prestonwood Baptist Church in Dallas, she has worked with women of all walks of life, ages, and stages. Her passion is to see modern and postmodern women connect, learn from one another, and bond around God's Word. Her Bible studies have ushered thousands of women all over the country and overseas into deeper Scripture study and community experiences.

With Kelley Mathews, Sue has coauthored *Organic Ministry to Women: A Guide to Transformational Ministry with Next Generation Women*; *Women's Retreats: A Creative Planning Guide*; and *Leading Women Who Wound: Strategies for an Effective Ministry*. Sue and Kelley joined with Henry Rogers to coauthor *Mixed Ministry: Working Together as Brothers and Sisters in an Oversexed Society*. *Organic Mentoring: A Mentor's Guide to Relationships with Next Generation Women*, coauthored with Barbara Neumann, explores the new values, preferences, and problems of the next generation and shows mentors how to avoid potential land mines and how to mentor successfully. Her newest book, *Invitation to Educational Ministry: Foundations of Transformative Christian Education*, coedited with George M. Hillman Jr., DTS vice president of education and professor of educational ministries and leadership, serves as a primary academic textbook for schools all over the country, as well as a handbook for church leaders.

Sue has a doctor of ministry degree from Gordon-Conwell Theological Seminary in Boston, a master's in Bible from Dallas Theological Seminary, and a bachelor's degree in journalism from Trinity University. With Dr. Joye Baker, she oversees the DTS doctor of educational ministries degree program, with a women-in-ministry emphasis.

Sue has been married to David forty-nine years. They have two married daughters, Heather and Rachel, and five grandchildren. David is a retired CAD applications engineer and a lay prison chaplain. Sue loves fine chocolates and exotic coffees, romping with her grandchildren, and taking walks with David and her two West Highland terriers, Quigley and Emma Jane.